# COMPENSATION PLANS
## *for Law Firms*
### Fourth Edition

Edited by James D. Cotterman
Altman Weil, Inc.

**ABA** LawPracticeManagementSection
MARKETING · MANAGEMENT · TECHNOLOGY · FINANCE

**Commitment to Quality:** The Law Practice Management Section is committed to quality in our publications. Our authors are experienced practitioners in their fields. Prior to publication, the contents of all our books are rigorously reviewed by experts to ensure the highest quality product and presentation. Because we are committed to serving our readers' needs, we welcome your feedback on how we can improve future editions of this book. We invite you to fill out and return the comment card at the back of this book.

Cover design by Andrew Alcala, ABA Publishing.

### Library of Congress Cataloging-in-Publication Data
Compensation Plans for Law Firms, Fourth Edition. James D. Cotterman, Editor: Library of Congress Cataloging-in-Publication Data is on file.

ISBN 1-59031-365-8

08 07 06 05 04   5 4 3 2 1

Discounts are available for books ordered in bulk. Special consideration is given to state bars, CLE programs, and other bar-related organizations. Inquire at Book Publishing, American Bar Association, 750 N. Lake Shore Drive, Chicago, Illinois 60611.

# Contents

# Acknowledgments

This manuscript was first prepared by Bob Weil of Altman Weil, Inc., and published by the American Bar Association Law Practice Management Section in 1986. It was substantially revised and expanded by lead author James D. Cotterman of Altman Weil and republished in 1995. A third edition was published in 2001. This fourth edition is created by James D. Cotterman, with assistance from Ward A. Bower, Thomas S. Clay, Alan R. Olson, James S. Wilber, and Peter A. Giuliani. Special thanks also go to JoAnn Miller and Anita Moore, whose efforts in bringing this endeavor together were important and much appreciated.

# *Letter to Readers*

As I reread my Letter to Readers for the third edition of this manuscript, it is startling to see how much our economy and our world has changed in three short years. In that letter I spoke of a robust, technology-driven economy, but cautioned that economies and labor markets experience both good and bad times. I admonished that the perks and dollars employers provided would not last. That said, I did not foresee how far reaching the events of the 1990s were or the depth of the implications for this decade.

We now live in a markedly different world and economy. Even as I write today in the fall of 2003, our economy presents a strange combination of positive factors—low inflation, low interest rates, high consumer spending, rising output, increasing productivity—coupled with declining employment and a now-receding concern over the possiblity of price deflation. I continue to hold the belief I put forth previously, ". . . economies and labor markets experience both good and bad times. When you consider that our nation has enjoyed a two-hundred-year run at an average 3.8 percent annual economic growth, it surely puts into perspective that 'up' cycles are longer, stronger, and more dynamic than 'down' cycles. Down cycles will come, and some may be deep and prolonged. But over the long term, we have proven capable of weathering such storms."

Just possibly we have learned a few important lessons. First, compensation is not a substitute for careful selection of the right people. Authors Jim Collins and David Maister make this point well in their texts *Good to Great* and *Practice What You Preach*, respectively. Second, there is no one best compensation system. Those same authors demonstrate with their research what I have maintained in this manuscript since 1995—the type of compensation system is not what makes the difference, but rather the decisions that the system produces and the people whom you choose to make the decisions for. Finally, we may be ready to raise the debate above the old adages "you get what you pay for" or "you get what you measure." While making great sound bites, such statements are a vast oversimplification of how organizations function or at least how the best organizations function.

The key strategy for those who are serious about improving performance is not to turn first to their compensation systems. The first thoughts should be about the people and the standards—are they the right people, and are they the right standards? Appendix 6 of this manuscript is possibly one of the more important articles on this topic for law firm managers to read and consider.

After that, it is time to consider how well your compensation decisions support your efforts. Compensation does not drive behavior; it supports management's efforts to get the best behaviors out of people. Do your compensation decisions build trust and credibility in the firm's leadership? If not, then explore what might be changed systemically, procedurally, or both.

*James D. Cotterman*

# About Altman Weil, Inc.

Altman Weil, Inc., provides consulting services to law firms; to the law departments of corporations, governmental agencies and not-for-profit organizations; to legal vendors; and to other organizations serving the legal profession. Founded in 1970, the firm is headquartered in Pennsylvania and assists clients located in the Americas, the European Union, Asia, and Australia.

The firm offers consulting services in the areas of strategy, management, marketing, organizational development, and operations. Specific assistance requested by our law firm clients includes management advisory services, governance and management structures, law firm mergers, practice management, branding, client relationships and performance feedback, capital structure, cost reduction, leadership, sales and management training, executive searches, technology strategy, and compensation. Increasingly we are called upon to assist with issues of productivity, owner admission criteria, succession, exit strategy, valuation, and sale of a practice.

Consulting services to our law department clients include strategic planning, organizational structure and development, benchmarking, best practices, client relations and services, client surveys, outside counsel selection, management and evaluation, compensation systems and structures, staffing, cost reduction and control, and strategic use of technology. Companies without in-house lawyers have retained the firm to conduct cost-benefit analyses to determine the need for a law department, as well as how to develop one.

Altman Weil Publications, Inc., publishes annually the *Survey of Law Firm Economics*, the Legal Assistant Management Association's *Annual Compensation Survey for Legal Assistants/Paralegals and Managers*, the *Law Department Compensation Benchmarking Survey*, and the *Law Department Management Benchmarks Survey*. Other regularly published studies include the *Compensation Systems in Private Law Firms Survey*, the *Managing Partner and Executive*

*Director Survey*, and the *Retirement and Withdrawal Survey for Private Law Firms*. Altman Weil also publishes a monthly newsletter, *Report to Legal Management*, and a monthly electronic advisory, *AWDirect*. Altman Weil continues to update its treatise on law office management, *How to Manage Your Law Office*, published by Matthew Bender & Co. At the invitation of the American Bar Association, its consultants have written various publications, including *Compensation Plans for Law Firms*.

The firm and its consultants have been recognized in major business publications, including *The Wall Street Journal*, *Time*, *U.S. News & World Report*, the *Economist*, *Forbes*, *Fortune*, the *New York Times*, *The Washington Post*, the *Globe and Mail* (Canada), the *Times* (London), and *USA Today*. Altman Weil consultants have authored articles for national and international legal publications including the *American Lawyer*, *ABA Journal*, *Law Practice*, *Legal Week*, *Commercial Lawyer*, and *International Financial Law Review*.

Altman Weil, Inc.
Suite 200
Two Campus Blvd.
Newtown Square, PA 19073
610-886-2000
**www.altmanweil.com**

# About the Editor

James D. Cotterman is a principal with Altman Weil, Inc. He joined Altman Weil in 1988 and advises clients on compensation, capital structure and other economic issues, governance, management, and law firm merger assessments.

Mr. Cotterman is a regular contributor to *The Altman Weil Report to Legal Management*, and has been the supervising author for Matthew Bender's loose-leaf text *How to Manage Your Law Office*. He is also a former member of the Board of Editors of *Accounting and Financial Planning for Law Firms*. His writings have appeared in the *American Lawyer,* the *National Law Journal, Law Practice Management, International Law Firm Management,* and other publications. Mr. Cotterman is a frequent speaker and lecturer including presentations for annual and regional conferences of the American Bar Association and the Association of Legal Administrators, as well as numerous state and local bar meetings.

Before joining Altma Weil, Mr. Cotterman was manager of acquisitions for a public company in the health care industry, where he developed, evaluated, negotiated, and integrated merger opportunities. His academic credentials include an undergraduate degree in operations management and an MBA in accounting, both from Syracuse University. Mr. Cotterman is a licensed Certified Public Accountant in the Commonwealth of Pennsylvania, and is a member of the American and Pennsylvania Institutes of Certified Public Accountants.

Mr. Cotterman can be reached at:

Altman Weil, Inc.
Suite 200
Two Campus Blvd.
Newtown Square, PA 19073
610-886-2011
**jdcotterman@altmanweil.com**

# Introduction

Compensation. Mention this word in almost any work setting and blood pressures rise, pulse rates quicken, defense mechanisms ready. Why? Compensation represents a tangible expression of a person's perceived value. It defines lifestyle; position within a community; status among peers, friends, and family; and it measures the relative importance of the individual to the organization. Compensation is one of the most complex and emotional issues that confront any business enterprise. Economics, psychology, sociology, politics, and ethics are all components in the compensation transaction.

Organizations continually work at "getting it right." The problem is that getting it right works only within the context of getting a whole lot of other things right. For example, compensation methodology must be *aligned* with the law firm's business objectives (its strategy). Compensation practices must be *aligned* with firm culture (its values and accepted behaviors). Firms that lack a clear understanding and agreement on these matters will surely have trouble getting the compensation process right. Finally, compensation decisions must be *aligned* with market reality for given skills and experience in a specific location. This relates to how profitable operations are achieved. Too many managers believe they overpay workers when, in reality, other factors inhibit organizations from achieving desired levels of profitability.

Each individual makes a personal judgment about the appropriateness (read fairness) of his or her compensation in two ways. First is the direct comparison with coworkers' compensation. In this instance, a large variation is often better accepted than a small difference. Second is the perceived economic comparison with others in the community. This is an analysis of lifestyle (home, cars, activities, and the like). Issues related to a perceived lack of fairness disrupt business objectives, cause employees to change jobs, and create despair. The potential damage these issues can wreak upon an organization overshadows most others.

A major reason free agency took hold of the legal profession was compensation. The legal market has been extremely competitive, and Model Rule 5.6 (formerly DR 2-108) effectively allows partners and shareholders in law firms to change firms and take their clients with them whenever they choose. Consequently, partners or shareholders with a book of business that would entitle them to significantly greater compensation elsewhere frequently leave their firms. The result is that the most productive partners or shareholders are tempted to defect—along with their revenue streams—placing a firm in severe jeopardy.

Make no mistake about the importance of compensation to the overall cost structure of a law firm. Of every fee dollar, 75 percent goes toward compensation in a law firm, be it partner compensation or associate and support staff salary and benefits. Compensation represents, in the aggregate, the largest and most significant set of transactions a law firm makes. Failure to attend properly to compensation issues can have disastrous consequences, including low productivity, high turnover, client dissatisfaction, low morale, and disputes with former partners and former and existing employees.

Law firms are closely held businesses with active owner participation. As such, any treatise on compensation for law firms must distinguish compensation systems for the active owners from compensation systems for the nonowner employees. Owner compensation is as much a political transaction as it is an exchange for services. Compensation for nonowners does not typically involve the political element. Although there are similarities between nonowner and owner compensation issues, the latter are fundamentally more complex.

This book is divided into five chapters that discuss compensation for the following groups:

1. Partners or shareholders
2. Of Counsel
3. Associates
4. Paraprofessionals
5. Staff

Retirement income is often considered an extension of the compensation package. In law firms, retirement income may include elements of a buy-out of an owner's interest, nonqualified deferred compensation arrangement, or income from qualified retirement plans. A primer on this topic appears in Appendix 3. The readers are also directed to another ABA publication, *Estate Planning Strategies: A Lawyer's Guide to Retirement and Lifetime Planning* for a more in-depth discussion of this topic.

Likewise, benefits occupy an important role in compensating employees. Today's benefits costs have escalated and can easily add 25 percent or more to the wages paid. Appendix 5 of this book provides basic guidelines and benchmarks for this area of compensation.

## Compensation Theory

Before examining compensation methodology, let's discuss compensation theory. Central to this topic is the concept of a labor market. A labor market is, in part, the geographic area from which a business is likely to employ workers. It also defines the area within which the business must establish its competitive position to attract and retain the caliber of worker desired. For example, hourly support staff (secretaries, receptionists, bookkeepers, clerks, and the like) normally are drawn from a very local market. They are unlikely to travel outside a well-defined and limited area to seek employment. Lawyers, however, are quite mobile and, subject to bar admission, can easily qualify to work in many jurisdictions. They represent a national—even international—labor market. A law firm from across the nation or around the globe can compete for a lawyer in your community.

Early in a lawyer's career, academic credentials significantly define the graduate's effective labor market. The reputation and prestige of the schools attended and the level of academic excellence achieved are important factors. Graduates from prestigious schools generally have opportunities anywhere in the country. Graduates from other schools may need to confine their searches to the geographic regions where their schools are well known, although school differences are shrinking.

As a lawyer is admitted to practice in one or more jurisdictions, gains experience, and specializes in an area of the law, an industry, or a geographic market for clients (Asia, for example), the labor market available to that lawyer changes. The market may be industry-related. For example, the tax laws for insurance companies are unlike the tax laws pertaining to almost all other companies. Consequently, the labor market for insurance-tax lawyers is different from the labor market for corporate-tax lawyers. The market may also cut across industries and relate to a practice area or practice segment. Patent lawyers tend to have technical specialties. The market for a patent lawyer with an organic chemistry background is likely to differ from the market for a patent lawyer with an electrical engineering background. The market for an international lawyer with an Asian focus is likely to differ from that of a lawyer with a Latin American or European focus.

As a lawyer matures in the profession, development of a client base may inhibit geographic opportunities. If a client base is global, the potential labor market and relocation opportunities may not be limited to any great extent. However, if the client base is regional or confined to a single state or limited to a specific community, the labor market is much narrower and opportunities to relocate are more limited.

Understanding the labor market in which a firm competes for talent, as well as the appropriate skill levels required, is central in making compensation decisions. If a firm competes in the national labor market, it must understand national compensation patterns. If it hires from a local market, national standards are less important; the firm must consider the prevailing local conditions.

Rarely are labor markets easily defined, discrete entities. They overlap. The various market-defining components of a position may operate in different labor markets. This concept can be illustrated with the Olympic symbol of interlocking rings.

## The Art and the Size of Compensation

Readers may look to this book for the magic answers to their compensation questions. Unfortunately, there are none. Effective decision making involves more art than science. An organization can get the job done right with a proper set of compensation tools: a methodology for making compensation decisions, a framework of criteria to apply, rational information on which to act, institutional knowledge of individuals and events, respected decision makers, and, finally, the skills to apply the tools, interpret the information against the criteria, and communicate the decisions. Doing the job right is no easy task.

A wise individual reminds us of the difficulty of achieving this goal. He says, "Most compensation schemes will result, *at best*, in an absence of perceived unfairness. It is like saying that the best society can do is avoid war. It is the lack of negative rather than the existence of positive that allows one to judge a compensation system as a success or failure. Toward this lack of negative, I believe numerical information must be used as a tool to support management compensation decisions made using an equal (or greater) amount of nonquantifiable factors. Numerical information should never determine or even drive those decisions; it should provide the empirical basis, which avoids potential mistakes and backs up the final decisions."[1]

Compensation methodologies can span a wide spectrum, from formulas to equal sharing to enlightened subjectivity. Any single, pure approach has weaknesses. With formulas, the great danger is believing that they can substitute for management decision making and can address all possible scenarios. Much time can be spent refining numbers to make a formula yield an acceptable result. The hidden obstacle in equal-sharing systems is in a means to change the percentages. People come and go, and relative internal allocations need to change over time. Generally, it is the difficulty in adopting those changes that causes problems with such systems. Enlightened subjectivity is often hampered by two events: lack of an accepted successor to an enlightened decision maker ("benevolent dictator") who steps down, and a perceived inconsistency between compensation decisions and generally circulated management data.

If there is a universal rule regarding compensation, it is this: every compensation system works, and every compensation system fails. Systems can run the spectrum from objective to subjective, participative to dictatorial. What works in a particular law firm is a system that fits the culture and strategy of the organization. That means that a good compensation system should be flexible; it should be able to survive evolving needs of the firm and produce decisions respected by those affected. A successful compensation system must be embraced by the partners and be consistent with their collective philosophy, background, and perspective.

Despite their differences, all successful compensation systems feature two linked, common qualities. First and foremost, a successful system is fair and perceived as fair by the partners who are essential to the firm's economic success and reputation. The perception of fairness is critical. Even a system that is objectively fair cannot survive if a substantial number of key players perceive it as unfair. Fairness should not be confused with satisfaction with one's own compensation. Fairness is measured by a sense of equity in the treatment of—and by—others. To determine the fairness of a compensation system, partners may want to ask themselves these questions:

- ◆ Do I understand the system?
- ◆ Does the system recognize what individuals contribute to the organization?
- ◆ Are the rules clear?
- ◆ Are the rules followed and applied in a consistent manner from person to person and from year to year?
- ◆ Are the compensation decision makers trusted and respected?

These questions define the perception of fairness. Partners observe the relative levels of compensation among them and determine the fairness of the system in the context of those questions.

A second quality of successful compensation systems is that of simplicity. Altman Weil's experience has shown that there is a direct correlation between the simplicity of a compensation system and the degree to which wage earners understand how their compensation is determined. That, in turn, goes a long way toward the perception of fairness. Simplicity is the foundation. For each additional consideration or step in a compensation system, one might ask, "Are we gaining sufficient additional information about an individual's contribution to make it worth the additional complexity?"

The difficulty in structuring a compensation system for a law firm is in selecting the best mix of compensable criteria and the right amount of participation, consistent with the firm's needs and its culture. A law firm evolves over time. Because of these changes, the compensation system must function like a good constitution—rules grounded in sound, basic principles and subject to amendment only after careful and thoughtful deliberation. The experience and objectivity of an expert outsider and the candor of confidential input often work together to maintain a desirable compensation system.

An important event in any law firm is the exchange of individual expectations regarding compensation:

- What are our objectives—formal or informal?
- How much money is enough?
- How much money is not enough?
- What does compensation mean, both personally and professionally, to each individual?
- What level of risk sharing should take place?
- How much disparity should exist from top to bottom?

These questions define much about how economic rewards can be fashioned and how they are divided among lawyers. They may even lead to a conclusion that there are partners and associates who should no longer be part of the firm.

An additional factor significant to compensation is that the legal profession is maturing, and the balance is shifting from the suppliers (lawyers) to the consumers (clients). The profession experienced an explosion in the number of lawyers, paralegals, and support personnel during the 1970s, 1980s, and 1990s. Positions that did not even exist in 1960 now have sophisticated trade associations—for example, legal administrators have the Association of Legal Administrators (ALA), legal assistants have the National Association of Legal Assistants (NALA), and marketing directors have the Legal Marketers Association (LMA). Information Systems (IS) or Information Technology (IT) directors now preside over the deployment of technology throughout law firms.

Concurrent with growth in the numbers of personnel has been an explosion in the starting salaries of new law school graduates. Nationally, new lawyers' starting salaries rose from a median of $14,000 in 1973 to a plateau of $50,000 in 1989.[2] That represented an increase of 257 percent, compared with a 184 percent increase in the consumer price index for the same period. Law firms then held the line on offers to recent graduates to a national median of $50,000 until 1995. In 1996, a small spike—to $52,000—occurred, and then the median returned to $50,000 in 1997. However, in 1998, law firms raised starting salaries 10 percent, to a national median of $55,000.[3] 1999 and 2000 saw the increases continue. In December 1999, a Silicon Valley law firm raised its starting salary to $125,000 with a guaranteed $20,000 bonus, and this was matched by many large-city firms in 2000. The national median starting salary in 2003 was just over $70,000.

Technology is just beginning to reshape the landscape for the delivery of legal services. The inroads to date, though impressive, have only touched the surface of what promises to be a fundamental shift. The implications of this shift are disruption, disequilibrium, and costly reorganization and investment. Couple this with aggressive pressure by clients to drive nonproductive costs out of their organizations, and the result is a legal market where vast changes are—and will be—taking place.

Illustration I.1 shows the change in relationships of compensation for four groups of lawyers, as compared with an index of compensation for recent law school graduates. This illustration sets median starting salaries of recent graduates at a constant value of 100 and relates the median earnings of other groups to that value. Comparisons are made for fifth-year associates, partners with nine years of experience, partners with between twenty-five and twenty-nine years of experience, and all partners as a group. In 1978, an experienced partner earned 4.7 times more than a new associate. The ratio generally declined until 1990, when it hit 3.6 (as the legal profession struggled with income

**ILLUSTRATION I.1**
**Relative Median Compensation Index of Lawyers in Private Practice**

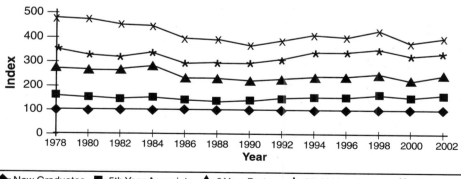

Source: 2003 *Survery of Law Firm Economics*, Altman Weil® Publications, Inc., Newtown Square, PA 19073.

compression and was on the verge of its own recession). By 1998 the ratio had improved to 4.3, only to fall back to 3.7 two years later. As of 2002, experienced partners earned 4.0 times more than a new associate.

Law is a very competitive profession. Even with the prosperous economic times, keeping good people is a challenge, as there always seems to be someone who is willing to pay more for the best people. Firms with less than stellar economics are hugely at risk for defections. This is because many of the problems in compensation systems, particularly owner compensation systems, relate not to the matter of income allocation, but to the overall economics of the practice. Often the compensation system is blamed when individual compensation is perceived as inadequate. But, with labor costs being such a significant component of law firm overhead, firm profitability is directly affected by each worker's compensation. In effectively dealing with problems in compensation systems, attention must be directed to the overall economics of a law firm's performance, as well as to the manner of income allocation.

Law firm owners must allocate limited economic resources among all the wage earners. As a consequence, there are no easy answers for compensation issues, and complete satisfaction is rarely possible. Firms must manage compensation risk, strive to attract and retain talented people, and stimulate them to pursue activities that contribute to the organization.

## Size and Compensation

It is generally accepted that firm size is important to potential partner income. There is some truth in this statement. According to Altman Weil's annual survey, the 2002 median compensation for equity partners was just under $163,000 in small firms and just under $327,000 in large firms (see Illustration I.2).

However, if one looks at the *American Lawyer 200* and compares firm size with compensation, a different picture emerges. These law firms (excluding one firm with over 1,800 lawyers and one firm with more than $2,000,000 in profits per equity partner) range in size from 140 lawyers to 1,700 lawyers. Average equity partner profits range from $280,000 to $2,000,000. The highest per-equity partner profits were in a firm that is 5 percent of the size of the largest firm. These were the two outliers excluded from the chart. Even when adjusted for outliers in firm size and profit per equity partner, there is little correlation in this group between size and per-partner profits (see Illustration I.3).

Size of firm had even less effect on a firm's ability to generate revenues per lawyer (see Illustration I.3.1).

## ILLUSTRATION I.2
## Median Equity Partner Compensation in 2002

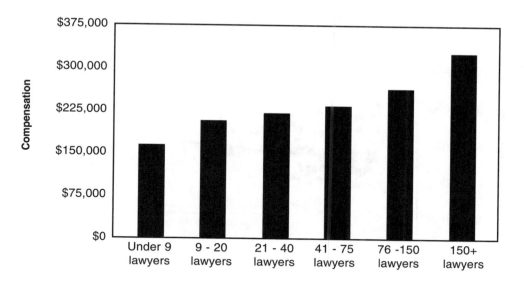

## ILLUSTRATION I.3
## 2003 AmLaw200: 2002 Profit Per Equity Partner/Size of Firm

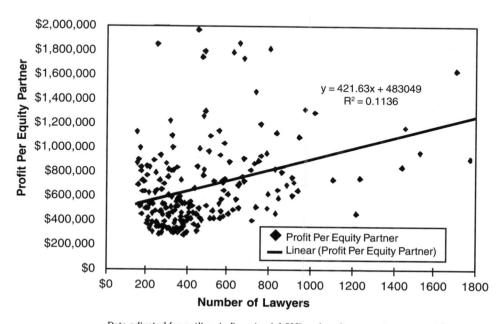

Data adjusted for outliers in firm size (>1,800) and profit per equity partner (>$2,000,000)
Source: American Lawyer Media

## ILLUSTRATION I.3.1
### 2003 AmLaw200: 2002 Revenue Per Lawyer/Size of Firm

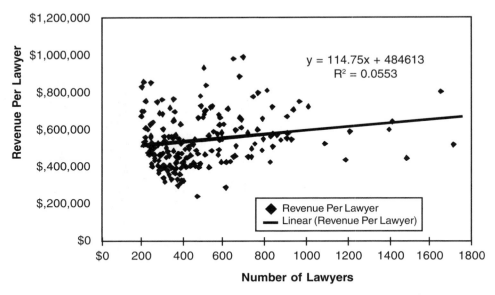

$$y = 114.75x + 484613$$
$$R^2 = 0.0553$$

Data adjusted for outliers in firm size (>1,800) and revenue per lawyer (>$1,000,000)
Source: American Lawyer Media

However, revenues per lawyer did correlate strongly with profits per equity partner (see Illustration I.3.2).

Let's extend that thinking and examine law firm profitability (see Illustration I.4).

The average 2002 firm income per lawyer (from Altman Weil's *Survey of Law Firm Economics*) was $154,000 in small firms and $275,000 in large firms. The chart resembles the partner compensation chart in Illustration I.2. If the most profitable 25 percent of firms in each size category are examined, the per-lawyer income ranges from $244,000 to $365,000 (see Illustration I.5), but it is not so nicely aligned with firm size. One should be careful not to assume that size is the only—or even inescapable—path to enhanced income.

## Payroll and Draw Cycles

The payroll cycle should be regular, balancing the needs of the law firm for efficient administration and the workers' needs for continuing cash flow. Payroll cycles can be weekly, biweekly (every other week—twenty-six times per year), semimonthly (twice a month—twenty-four times per year), or monthly. Some firms have alternating payrolls to even out cash flow. An example is al-

## ILLUSTRATION I.3.2
## 2003 AmLaw200: 2002 Profit Per Equity Partner/Revenue Per Lawyer

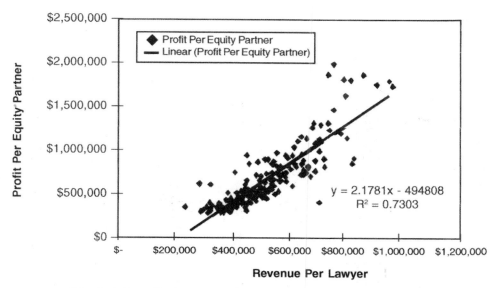

Data adjusted for outliers in revenue per lawyer (>1,000,000) and profit per equity partner (>$2,000,000)
Source: American Lawyer Media

## ILLUSTRATION I.4
## Average Per Lawyer Firm Income in 2002

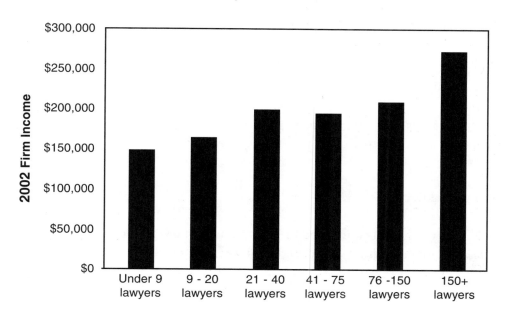

**ILLUSTRATION I.5**
**Most Profitable 25% of Firms: Per Lawyer Firm Income in 2002**

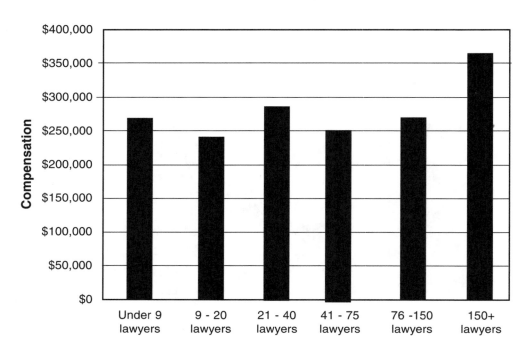

ternating biweekly payrolls, with all staff and associates on one cycle and partners on the other. This works to smooth out cash flow, but it may add to the firm's bookkeeping burdens.

Generally, support staff, who are paid less and sometimes live from paycheck to paycheck, prefer a weekly or biweekly cycle. Semimonthly and monthly cycles have occasional extra weekends that slip into the pay period, just as employers have two or four months during the year in which an extra payroll falls. It is more of a hardship for lower-income employees to plan for such occurrences than it is for the firm to plan for its extra cycles. Generally, most firms use a semimonthly or monthly cycle for owners, and either a biweekly or semimonthly cycle for everyone else.

## Survey Data

In 2003, Altman Weil conducted its fourth study of law firm compensation systems. Summary information from that study (*Compensation Systems in Private Law Firms Survey*) is used throughout this book, as is summary information taken from Altman Weil's annual *Survey of Law Firm Economics*, and Altman

Weil's triennial surveys, *Retirement and Withdrawal for Private Law Firms* and *Managing Partner and Executive Director Survey.*

## Endnotes

1. Conversation with Robert M. Schack.

2. *Survey of Law Firm Economics* (Newtown Square, PA: Altman Weil Publications, Inc., various years).

3. Ibid.

# Partner and Shareholder Compensation

## Overview

The form of organization selected by a law firm has significant impact on the tax consequences of its compensation system. It is largely irrelevant, however, in connection with the principles used to determine compensation within a law firm. For the purpose of this discussion, salary and draw will be interchangeable terms, as will bonus and distribution. Documentation differences are very important because of the need to ensure the desired tax consequence of these transactions. Differences in compensation methodology between partnerships and professional corporations are, therefore, primarily driven by the tax treatments the firms and their owners receive.

Devising a compensation program for the owners is, by far, the most difficult compensation-related task. Owners must deal from "inside the circle" on this issue. Associates, of counsel, and staff are all external groups and generally do not have the same level of risk-associated attributes in their compensation as do owners.

Owner compensation must address several issues. First is remuneration for the fair value of an individual's contributions. Second is the recognition and provision of a return on invested capital. Third is generation of profits that are shared in some manner by the owners. This is an issue peculiar to a closely held business, where the owners are active in day-to-day affairs. Many compensation systems try to address all three issues from an undivided pool of money. In a manufacturing setting, there is much guidance concerning the relationship between the value for work rendered and the return on invested capital; in a law firm, such guidance is largely unavailable.

# Partner and Shareholder Compensation Criteria

The following unranked attributes regarding law firm owner compensation criteria should assist readers in positioning their own experiences. If your firm's experience is not consistent with the generalities and the system is working, then do nothing. If the system is not working, then look for differences and see if they offer some direction.

## Ownership

Partners or shareholders, as owners of an enterprise, are entitled to some reward for their investment and risk. The owners of a law firm are, after all, entrepreneurs. They meet a payroll, accept liability for the firm's activities, and provide capital. The most important asset of a law firm, however, is its client base, and clients cannot be owned or sold. The courts have consistently upheld the client's ultimate right to choose legal representation as a matter of public interest and policy. However, it is possible for a practice to be transferred for consideration. The ABA and most states have set forth guidelines involving such transactions that go beyond the scope of this text. However, at this writing, there is a very practical limit to the value of ownership.

Some law firms pay interest on capital invested in the firm as a way to reward ownership or to provide a return appropriate to the level of capital invested. In professional corporations, owner capital can be structured as a combination of equity and debt such that a return (interest) is paid on the debt. Although dividends can be declared and paid on equity, it is not tax efficient to do so. This is probably the easiest and best method to handle a return on invested capital. It removes return on capital from the compensation decision, allowing the owners to compensate for an individual's contribution and to allocate the profits generated by others among the owners.

Law firms have generally separated compensation from ownership. That is, relative compensation levels do not affect or track relative levels of ownership. This should always be true for those lawyers practicing in professional corporations, to avoid treatment of compensation as dividends, subjecting all or part of it to double taxation. Partnerships have also determined that compensation and ownership can evolve on separate tracks. However, the topic of allocating ownership interests can be as significant an issue as compensation. Ownership is now viewed as a means to apportion the owner capital needs of the organization and to establish certain voting rights in the governance of the firm's affairs. The level of importance accorded ownership in compensation has decreased.

## *Seniority*

Although some firms are entirely structured around length of service in the profession and in the firm, this factor has declined in importance for most law firms in compensation decisions. This came about primarily because of the increasingly competitive nature of the profession.

However, a key aspect of the strength of any organization is its heritage and stability. For law firms that have sought to preserve or regain these characteristics, tenure is accorded some significance. These features are gaining increasing importance, not only to clients who quickly tire of following their lawyers from firm to firm, but also to lenders and landlords who recognize the importance of those traits in securing the repayment of long-term obligations. Insurance underwriters are also aware of the importance of career association with a single firm in the prevention of errors and omissions.

Although respondents in the Altman Weil compensation systems study[1] indicated that years of experience as a practicing lawyer was the least-considered factor in owner compensation, there remains a strong correlation between years of experience and compensation, which is driven in part by economics (higher billing rates and greater efficiency of experienced fee producers) and by traditional notions of progressive compensation over a career. Illustration 1.1 depicts the general trend of compensation throughout a

**ILLUSTRATION 1.1**
**Total Compensation—All Partners/Shareholders**
**(By years since admission to the Bar, all firms 2002)**

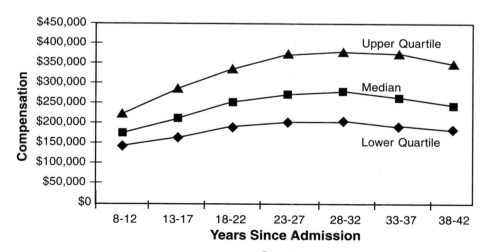

Source: 2003 *Survey of Law Firm Economics*, Altman Weil® Publications, Inc., Newtown Square, PA 19073.

partner's career. Generally, a partner's earnings peak around the thirtieth year of practice.

Seniority encompasses more than just a person's age or the number of years he or she has spent at a firm. One New England partnership broadly defined seniority to include the "number of years the partner has spent developing and maintaining clients, building and enhancing the firm's reputation, and participating in the training and development of a cadre of lawyers who produce for the benefit of all the partners in the firm."

### Pro Bono

Pro bono and similar nonbillable activities generally are of little importance in compensation. Such endeavors do not translate into fee receipts within the very short-term orientation many partners have regarding profitability. Often overlooked is the benefit gained, individually and organizationally, when one gives back to the profession and community. Provided the efforts are not overdone and the firm coordinates and approves the activities, they should be considered when compensation is determined.

### Teaching, Writing, and Speaking

Often lawyers give back to their profession by assisting in the educational process of other lawyers. They may teach continuing legal education classes or lecture at law schools. They may write for legal journals or speak at bar association meetings. Aside from the obvious benefit of enhancing the knowledge level of the profession, such activities allow individuals to establish credentials as experts in selected areas of the law. Some firms choose to reward these endeavors.

### Collegiality and Team Play

Collegiality is adherence to the spirit, as well as to the letter, of firm policies, a willingness to pitch in when needed, the sense of working and getting along together in a spirit of cooperation, a mutual respect for others' skills, and tolerance for others' weaknesses. It is important to those firms seeking to foster a team orientation. Practicing law is stressful enough—a firm does not need the added stress of "lone rangers" (that is, inconsiderate tyrants or abusive egotists). Contributions toward internal harmony—a sense that the firm will pull together to meet the challenges and demands facing it—are gaining in importance in compensation decisions.

### Training

Law firms engage in an ongoing process of inducting new members (lawyers, paralegals, and staff) into the organization and integrating them into the work system. In team-oriented firms, such integration is essential and valued accordingly. Because law firms make substantial investments in finding and pay-ing new lawyers and staff, and because the quality of supervision, training, and monitoring that inexperienced individuals receive is of significant impor-tance to their development and the quality of service provided to clients, law firms must be prepared to pay the trainers.

## Expertise

Expertise in a specialty or in some facet of professional activity can add to an individual's value as a partner. If a law firm needs the services of a specialist to advertise itself as qualified, the capabilities of that specialist may offset some lack of fee receipts or direct client development.

Legal expertise is most broadly defined as the quality and efficiency of work product and advice, particularly if the expertise is outstanding and the lawyer serves as a resource for others within the firm and legal community. Someone once said he could not define quality, but could identify unaccept-able work product, service, or advice. The following definition, used by a client of Altman Weil, conveys the concept well: "Quality includes knowledge of applicable law, imagination, creativity, and innovation; the ability to write clearly and persuasively; the ability to analyze quickly and accurately; the ability to exercise good judgment; the ability to plan and implement legal strategies; good oral communication skills; the ability to handle the unex-pected; the ability to negotiate; and the ability to handle complex matters."

## Leadership and Management

In industrial and business settings, management is paid more highly than pro-duction, and sometimes more highly than sales, although not necessarily so. Many law firms do not pay for management at all. Illustration 1.2 shows the relative earnings of the highest-paid partner, average partner, lowest-paid partner, and managing partner. Generally, if a law firm does not pay for man-agement, it will have little, because free work is grudgingly given. Firm-ap-proved budgets, combined with documented duties and authority, provide a framework for compensation considerations. Over the five-year interval be-tween the two studies, managing partner compensation improved relative to their counterparts.

Firm management (defined as contribution to firm, office, or practice management, including services such as acting as the firm's managing part-ner, serving on committees, chairing a department or practice area, recruiting and training professional employees, and the like) is a necessary and impor-tant function in any modern law firm. Good management requires time and ef-fort—the same time and effort one would otherwise devote to fee-paying clients.[2] A firm's recognition of the importance of management and the sacri-fices made by good managers is crucial.

**ILLUSTRATION 1.2**
**Relative Average Compensation**

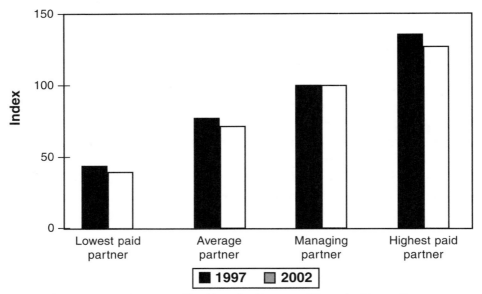

Source: 1997 and 2002 *Law Firm Managing Partner and Executive Director Survey*,
Altman Weil® Publications, Inc., Newtown Square, PA 19073.

As firms grow, management becomes more centralized. This is necessary to carry out the firm's functions in an orderly manner. Centralizing management responsibilities in one person or a few people requires reducing the contributions of such persons elsewhere. This is especially true for managing partners. Compensation issues arise not only in valuing the management contributions of a sitting managing partner, but also in determining compensation during the transition from management back into practice or retirement.

Many managing partners have devoted years tending to a firm's welfare. Illustrations 1.3 and 1.3.1 depict how the typical managing partner's time is allocated.

Clearly, generating more fees as a working lawyer has captured the attention of managing partners, possibly at a time when good management was never more desperately needed. When it comes time to turn over the reins of authority, managers often find that they have watched (and assisted in) the transfer of their practices to other firm members—accordingly, their practices have become substantially reduced. They may be only sixty years old (or younger), and they do not look fondly upon rebuilding a practice. Firms must consider this typical scenario and provide for "rough justice" in dealing with the postmanagement period. Failure to do so makes it harder to get senior management to depart when that becomes necessary, and sends the best of the next generation running for cover.

## ILLUSTRATION 1.3
### How Managing Partners Spent Their Time in 1997

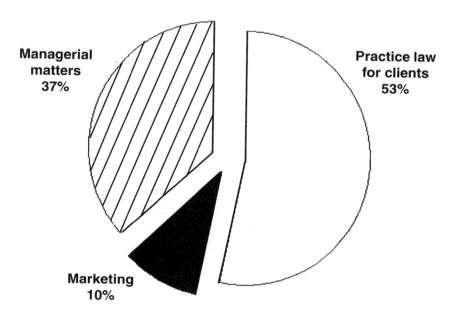

Source: 1997 *Law Firm Managing Partner and Executive Director Survey*, Altman Weil® Publications, Inc., Newtown Square, PA 19073.

## ILLUSTRATION 1.3.1
### How Managing Partners Spent Their Time in 2002

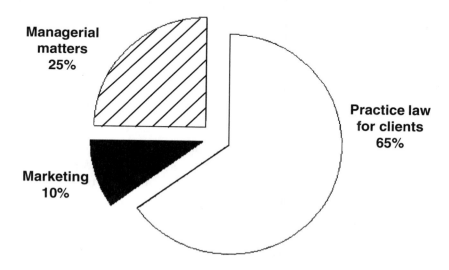

Source: 2002 *Law Firm Managing Partner and Executive Director Survey*, Altman Weil® Publications, Inc., Newtown Square, PA 19073.

### Fees Collected

Fees collected for personal work performed was the most important factor formally considered by respondents in the study.[3] Law firms must have a complement of fully utilized fee producers. This includes the partners, who also serve as managers, originators (sales), and owners (risk takers). Although a partner's compensation is not necessarily limited to the amount of his or her work that is billed and collected, a partner's work can have a considerable effect upon the economic results of a firm. This is, of course, more true in smaller organizations than in larger firms. Often overlooked, but an important consideration, is the impact of work performed that is not billed or collected, unless it represented pro bono work and was performed in accordance with firm policy.

Law firms have moved toward measuring fee collections through objective criteria such as working-lawyer productivity, billing-lawyer productivity, origination, and portfolio responsibility. Hours or billings fall short for partners, because their responsibility does not end until the bills are paid.

### Client Retention

Client retention is often defined as including both client responsibility (a lawyer's maintenance of good client relations and service, even if little work is actually performed by that lawyer), and case responsibility (delegation and direction of others' efforts, to obtain the best possible results for the client). Responsibility for maintaining the existing client and growing that client's business is acknowledged as an important element for survival in a competitive market. Many law firms reward the billing partner or responsible partner for this client retention function based on fee collections from work done by others. Such reward is often separate from the traditional origination or sales function.

### Origination and Sales

The one single factor that establishes the life or death of a law firm is its client base. The rainmakers—the people who acquire and cultivate client relationships—are the lifeblood of an organization. The true rainmakers are likely to be the highest-paid individuals in any organization. The ability to develop and maintain client relationships that serve as a conduit for work coming into the firm is the skill that establishes authority, power, and independence within a law firm. Those lawyers are the net exporters of work to others in the firm. There may be no more important decision for law firms today than judging this skill and doing so accurately for promotion and compensation decisions. It has been and continues to be either the number one or number two[4] objective criterion in partner compensation systems. The other criterion is personal productivity measured as fees collected as a working lawyer (see above).

Formal origination credit systems are used in 46 percent of law firms overall, but are far more likely to be found in large law firms (72 percent). This should not be surprising as small firm partners are more likely to have an intuitive grasp of where and how business is generated than do the compensation committees of large law firms. When formal credit systems are used, many will ask for how long a partner should expect to retain the credit. Much has been written about the need to "sunset" origination—that is, individual attribution becomes firm attribution after some period of time. The argument in favor of this position states that after a period of years, many lawyers within the firm service most clients, and the reason that a client continues with the firm is due to collective, not individual, effort. In such firms, the origination credit may reduce much the way an insurance sales commission reduces to a very small annuity. In others, the credit vanishes or is awarded to a department, office, or the firm. Sometimes a management credit is awarded to those responsible for maintaining a current relationship. A sunset provision also provides an incentive to go out and bring more new business to the firm. Many a firm has wrestled with the partner who retired on origination annuities, which is sometimes exacerbated when the partner can't remember the names of the clients! However, the data suggests that firms have overwhelmingly adopted the view that origination runs with the client as long as the client is with the firm (77 percent of firms allocate origination on this basis).[5]

This view is probably more consistent with the marketplace perspective that origination belongs to those who hold the relationships that bind the client. This view can foster destructive behavior if taken to an extreme. Management must foster a culture and recognize behaviors that create broader and more in-depth relationships between firms and their clients to mitigate that behavior.

### Participation in Community and Bar Activities

Lawyers are visible members of their communities. Notoriety is achieved through press reports on lawyers' courtroom skills and engagements in the political arena. Visibility is also achieved through lawyers' contributions to civic, volunteer, charitable, community, and religious organizations, and similar activities. Such efforts certainly enhance the community; they also elevate the image of the lawyers' firms, while simultaneously polishing the subtle, yet important, leadership skills of the lawyers.

In law firms that foster strong feelings of obligation to the law as a profession, credit may be given for participation in local, state, or national bar association work.

Many law firms recognize the importance of these activities, through support of individual participation and through compensation. Law is a business of people. For the most part, clients engage individual lawyers, and the means to that engagement is often through relationships established outside the traditional office setting. Also, some firms with specialty practices, which rely heavily on referral work from lawyers, attribute much of the referral work to the friendships that develop as a result of bar association work.

Some law firms look favorably on above-average contribution in these areas and recognize it in their pay plans, some regard it as an obligation meriting no special credit, and a few actually penalize excessive contribution, although they would not be likely to say so.

## Profitability

Increasingly, law firms examine the profitability of their client portfolios. Such examinations obviously look at the revenues generated against the overhead and resources required to service the work. In addition, strategic plans and marketing plans come into play, as some work is critical in the context of overall firm strategy. Selected matters, practice areas, and clients may support or enable other more lucrative services and must be evaluated accordingly.

A second aspect of profitability involves the acceptance of clients and matters and the fee structures set up to service the work. In a competitive environment, there is significant pressure to keep the timekeepers fully utilized. It may appear advantageous to accept all work; however, work for which a firm cannot bill or collect fees has limited value. Some make the argument that in pricing initial work, short-term investments in a client are useful to getting a foot in the door, though at some point this investment must show a return. Others conclude that pricing initial legal services is like negotiating a starting salary—it's best to get the amount as high as possible, because you are establishing a baseline that will stay with you for a long time.

Yet another aspect of profitability encompasses the stewardship of partners with billing responsibilities over work-in-progress and accounts receivable. Two measurements are important in this regard. The age of the asset and realization (the percentage of the asset ultimately converted into cash) must be examined in tandem. These assets are not like fine red wines that improve with age. Collections, and therefore realization, are improved with frequent, timely bills and diligent follow-up for bills over thirty days old.

Action—or inaction—in these areas can affect every partner's income. The definition of profitability and its measurement can be difficult issues on which to reach consensus among partners. Therefore, movement in that direction has been slow.

## Quality

Some lawyers view quality as a standard inherent in the credentials required to practice law. Others say that quality is an ethical requirement that is the responsibility of each lawyer. Yet others say that quality embodies more than just the standards of the profession—it is also defined by the client.

Quality in the delivery of legal services is undergoing a metamorphosis. A complete discussion of the movement of quality programs through law firms and their clients is outside the scope of this text. However, it should be noted that such programs have importance to the legal profession. Law firms and their clients continue to explore alternatives in the pricing of legal services, the delivery of legal services, and training methods, among other areas. By definition, such programs are never fully implemented or completed. The overriding goal is continuous improvement, requiring that the search for quality improvement focus on increasingly smaller increments.

For those firms considering or engaged in quality programs, the issue of quality in compensation decisions must be addressed. Compensating excellence in providing high-quality work product, advice, and service to clients is in keeping with the results that clients desire, as opposed to measuring productivity (fees, hours, and the like), which is generally inconsistent with clients' objectives. As law firms develop partnering relationships with clients, such compensation philosophies will increase in importance.

## *Productivity*

Productivity describes the totality of a partner's contributions to a firm and its clients. Partner productivity goes beyond the numbers generated from the firm's time and billing system. It includes the efficiency with which assignments are carried out, the quantity and complexity of work handled, the number of lawyers supervised, the time invested in training, and other firm activities. Assessing productivity means viewing a multitude of issues in addition to hours and fees. Another term gaining in use, with a similar meaning, is total contribution.

The compensation criteria described above can be brought together in a tangible way through individual business plans. Each partner defines what he or she will contribute to the firm in the coming year. Individual plans can be rolled up into practice, office, and firm plans, thereby ensuring consistency, reasonableness, and alignment with the overall strategy. In each case the plan should set forth specific objectives, milestones for measuring achievement, resources required, and the like. Management must ensure that the plans are balanced, that the plans utilize individual strengths, that the plans create appropriate stretch in performance, and that opportunities to work together are identified.

For compensation purposes, the plans serve as a foundation to review performance—holding individuals accountable for their stated actions while acknowledging the inevitable changes that come about during implementation. Compensation decision makers may consider how much was accomplished, how well it was done, how unforeseen challenges were addressed, and how unexpected new opportunities were accommodated. Such consideration can affect year-end bonus or distribution, or next year's salary or draw. Point, percentage, and lockstep progression can be similarly affected.

The use of individualized plans can, therefore, create a planning mechanism, a performance evaluation tool, an input into the compensation decision process, and a learning tool for future planning.

## Classes of Partners

Multilevel ownership structures are a significant aspect of large law firm ownership structures. They are much less prevalent in smaller law firms (see Table 1.1). Understanding who should be full equity and who should be some other tier of ownership is a very important consideration. Making the right choices here is good for the firm long-term and facilitates rational compensation systems and decisions.

**TABLE 1.1**
**Existence of Second Class of Partners/Shareholders**

|  | *By Selected Firm Sizes* | *All Firms* |
|---|---|---|
| 2–9 Lawyers | 100+ Lawyers |  |
| 16% | 66% | 31% |

Source: *COMPENSATION SYSTEMS IN PRIVATE LAW FIRMS SURVEY* (Newtown Square, PA: Altman Weil Publications, Inc., 1997), 40.

The authors' consulting experience leads to a caution: when lawyers are placed permanently into special, lower-prestige categories, morale problems invariably result over the years. Establishing a lower class of partners as an intermediate step for a limited number of years is often preferable. However, given the economic changes in the profession, some lawyers may never achieve the distinction of full ownership. As long as the barrier is established on legitimate criteria that are fairly administered, such an outcome should have minimal adverse consequences.

## Administration of the Compensation Process

After selecting the criteria for compensation of owners, the firm must devise a plan for administering the compensation process.

Owners at many smaller firms still sit down and discuss an equitable distribution of the pie at year-end, either prospectively or retrospectively. Each partner participates in the meeting at which voting on income distribution occurs. Because lawyers are generally reluctant to discuss each other's strengths and weaknesses in a face-to-face setting, systems administered by the firm as a whole tend to be quite similar to the lockstep described hereafter. Quite often, partners find such meetings uncomfortable and stressful. It is not the inclination of many lawyers to participate actively in open review meetings; therefore, some firms use closed peer reviews with written evaluations. This method is one way of allowing broad input into a process that works well in many small firms.

Large firms often find such meetings and formal partner peer reviews awkward and time consuming (although some pursue this course if it is in keeping with their culture). As firm size increases, so does the use of compensation committees. In some firms, management designates a compensation committee. Other firms hold general elections. A few partnership agreements specify the makeup of compensation committees. Each method has its place, depending on the personalities involved.

In large firms, such committees make use of input from managing partners, department chairs, and practice managers to help assess individual contributions. This is consistent with the objective of aligning management functions with compensation decisions. Involving managers in this way strengthens their abilities to reinforce the behaviors they seek to instill.

Compensation committees are used by almost half the participants in the Altman Weil survey, which shows that the typical compensation committee has three to seven individuals (varying principally by size of firm) elected by the partners for two to three years each and who can succeed themselves.[6] It is most important that the firm elect individuals who place the firm's interests above their own. Compensation committees are almost as likely to make final decisions as they are to make recommendations to the partners.

The compensation process is largely a participative event. Compensation committees spend much of their time hearing from their partners either by personal interviews, written submissions, or both before decisions are reached. Although a time-consuming process, many believe the benefits gained in credibility and understanding greatly outweigh the costs. Now more firms are focusing on postdecision interviews as a means to communicate the rationale of their decisions. This step improves the likelihood that the compensation message is accurately received.

A few firms charge a senior partner with the responsibility of proposing a distribution of income for each year. Either a governing committee or the firm as a whole generally reviews this proposal, but typically it is not changed. Given the right complement of partners, this system works well.

An alternative method, which avoids confrontations, is the mutual rating system. In this process, income allocations—either in points or percentages—

are made by secret ballot of the partners. A neutral party, such as the firm's accountant, compiles the ballots. In some cases, the high and low ratings are disregarded and the remaining ballots are averaged. Experience indicates that this process often becomes a proxy for a lockstep system, but not always. The major disadvantage of the system is that adversely rated partners often do not know why they are adversely rated, because there is no feedback. Consequently, the compensation system cannot be used to correct perceived flaws or problems in the activities of partners who are not rated well. This rating process is obviously political, which means that partners could be rewarded for their popularity rather than their productivity. Partners who consistently fare poorly in such a process often leave their firms.

A few firms have abandoned the annual compensation ritual, choosing instead to review compensation on a biennial or triennial basis. Such a review period is almost always acceptable to senior partners and unacceptable to junior partners, who look for strong annual growth in earnings. A reason for using this method is to allow for a greater interval of time to elapse, thus forcing compensation decision-makers to consider longer-term contributions.

### Practice Area Considerations

Practice-specific differences exist. For example, many intellectual property firms gravitate toward the formulaic and objective end of the spectrum, due mostly to the lawyers' scientific disciplines and facility with numbers. Insurance defense firms have unique institutional client relationships that require compensable criteria that differ from criteria in a transactional practice. Plaintiffs' litigation firms, though transactional, tend to be boutiques, and exhibit high entrepreneurial orientation that needs to be recognized.

### Determining Compensation Structure

A firm that sees a need to change its compensation system recognizes the dangers of the status quo. Key business developers may take clients and leave, or highly talented, technically skilled lawyers may be bought at auction. The effect is a loss to the organization and a disruption in the lives and livelihoods of the remaining members. At the same time, the firm perceives danger in internally induced change—in any closed economic system, a change in compensation results in some people getting less, while others take more. This perceived danger could block compensation reform within the firm. Prospective change and transition become key elements in the evolution of a compensation system. Change needs to be prospective—looking forward, and providing time for the players to adjust to a new set of rules. Many firms also take specific action to prevent massive annual reduction in compensation under a new system. Limits on downward revisions are enacted to protect individual economic circumstances. This step is a major consideration and selling point to mollify insecure partners. Often, two, three, or more years may be required to move from an existing system to a new system.

The nature of compensation makes selection of compensable criteria difficult. A successful law firm needs all the qualities that the various criteria attempt to measure. As always, the individual characteristics of the firm dictate how to blend the ingredients into a successful compensation system. It is possible to reduce the emotion and stress inherent in compensation by understanding that precision and absolute correctness are not attainable. At best, one can create a sense of rough justice, wherein the essential partners are satisfied with the system's fairness, appreciative of the simplicity, and motivated to work.

Reginald Heber Smith, in a series of articles published in the *American Bar Association Journal* in 1940, defined the objectives of a profit-division plan: "The whole purpose is to let the work in the office flow where it will be done best, most quickly, and at lowest cost. The lawyer having too much business must not be afraid to part with it. He must be encouraged to do so, [and] the system must protect his natural and proper interest in the case and the fruits thereof."[7] The objectives of Smith's system, which was installed at the Boston firm of Hale & Dorr, were to ensure specialization and profitability, and also to reward the individual who was perceived to have an interest in the case. Not all firms would agree with all these objectives. Further, there is evidence that the statistical system, devised by Smith and discussed later, may work against specialization in some circumstances when it is not installed in the same way as it was under Smith's leadership and guidance.

## Type of Organization

Relatively little thought is given to the fundamental attitudes that determine how lawyers organize themselves as a group. But the attitudes or views of individual lawyers in the practice shape all facets of behavior—particularly compensation.

Many people who enter law school choose the law as a career because they are independent and value personal achievement. Their college and law school training reinforces individual competitiveness and the ability to master situations independently. When lawyers first enter smaller law firms, they are generally given responsibilities after a short time and they may receive guidance and training only when they seek it. This freedom reinforces an independent attitude. It is no wonder, therefore, that many organizations of lawyers function as loose confederations of individuals, rather than as organized, disciplined teams. Many lawyers have never considered practicing as part of a true team, nor have they considered the ramifications of association with a team or confederation type of organization, particularly in connection with compensation.

As it relates to compensation, whether a firm operates as a team or con-federation is largely a matter of degree. The pure team (equal division of prof-its) and the pure confederation (space sharers only) are rare.

***Confederation.***    In a confederation law practice, each lawyer develops individual client relationships. Quite often, there is subtle competition for clients within the office, because serving the more important or better-paying clients provides direct rewards and advancement.

Many lawyers are happy only in a confederation environment. They enjoy the sense of independence and the lack of accountability that this or-ganization makes possible. In a confederation, each lawyer is viewed as a mas-ter of his or her craft and is permitted to practice with little supervision or ac-countability. The office exists merely to facilitate each lawyer's practice. It provides staff support, a library, occasional research assistance and similar amenities, coverage during absence or illness, and companionship. The office, while providing many important aids, is not central to the work the lawyer performs for clients. There is no need for substantial collaboration or coop-eration among lawyers.

This form of organization has some obvious shortcomings. There is no central strategy for attracting work. Professional resources may not be opti-mally used, and specialization is generally neglected. There is a lack of high-quality review. Training is often a stepchild. There is usually little standardi-zation of forms and work habits, because essentially each lawyer practices alone.

In a confederation, one is most likely to find a compensation plan based on measures of work production and client origination, which are described later.

***Team.***    In a team practice, lawyers serve clients by working collabora-tively as a single entity, rather than as a collection of individuals. This ap-proach to practice requires the subordination of lawyers' individual egos to two principles: clients are better served by lawyers who are, at least to a de-gree, specialized, and the lawyers in the firm are all, in their own areas, com-petent to serve any client. Team-oriented firms generally have well-defined specializations and a view of clients as belonging to the firm rather than to any individual partner.

Many large law firms adopt some variation of the team approach, because the many facets of legal matters handled are too demanding for individual lawyers to manage alone. But the team approach is available for small firms as well. In the smallest group practice—that of two lawyers—the team approach may be manifested by one partner doing all the litigation and the other concentrating on office work, to the extent that workloads permit. Somewhat larger team firms are generally organized so that all tax, probate, and estate planning matters are handled by specified individuals, all litigation is concentrated elsewhere, all real estate served by specialists in that field, and corporate matters handled by other lawyers. A full-service (to borrow a phrase from commercial banks) law firm must be organized in the team fashion.

Generally, team firms do not divide income on a purely statistical basis (work produced and clients obtained), although they may require that members work a certain quota of productive hours. Team firms typically set firm-wide standards for the acceptance of assignments, and, relative to confederation firms, share support staff more easily and manage members of the firm more closely. Today, team firms also develop firm-wide marketing and strategic plans to further the interests of the organization. These strategies call upon all the talent available within a firm and use each talent to the firm's best advantage.

### Prospective or Retrospective Orientation

Overall, U.S. law firms use a retrospective—or combination retrospective and prospective—approach when making compensation decisions, according to data from Altman Weil's study of compensation systems.[8]

In a prospective system, shares are determined at or before the beginning of a year and apply to that upcoming year. A partner will know his or her share of the pie, but not the size (value) of the share. Everyone has a common incentive to work hard to increase profits, because doing so increases the value of each share. The use of this mechanism has decreased over the past five years, primarily because of an increased use of incentive plans that require retrospective consideration.

In a retrospective system, partners' interests are determined at year-end or shortly thereafter. Unfortunately, it has been the authors' experience that these partners have sometimes been unable to file income tax returns on a timely basis, because their compensation for the prior year had not been resolved. Shareholders in a professional corporation do not have this problem, as they incur a significant tax cost as a penalty for not arriving at an amicable decision before the end of a fiscal year. The key advantage to a retrospective system is that it allows a firm to reward superior performance when the money is available. It also provides a tool to lower a partner's compensation if performance lags. Law firms with irregular cash flow are particularly more likely to use retrospective determination of partners' interests.

Many firms prefer to mix these perspectives. A partner's salary or draw may be set at the beginning of the year (prospective view), considering long-term performance. At year-end, profits exceeding base compensation are divided by looking back at performance during the year (retrospective view), with heavy weight on a single year's performance.

## Profit Centers

Law firms are realizing that practices and clients, like lawyers, do not contribute equally to the bottom line. Some firms have drilled down to the lowest common denominator—the individual worker or client—while others stay at an office, practice area, department, or client industry level. Such measurement tools may also be used to evaluate offices during a merger or the establishment of a new office. The most common pitfall in the use of profit centers is that individuals measure the wrong criteria, resulting in the wrong actions.

A profit center approach uses cost accounting principles to allocate revenue and expense to individual offices, practice areas, clients, and (sometimes) timekeepers. The accounting systems of most law firms are not well designed for cost accounting. The more sophisticated systems are better, but involve substantially greater cost and difficulty in implementation. Several sources should be part of a reading library on the topic of profit center accounting:

- ◆ *Results-Oriented Financial Management: A Step-By-Step Guide to Law Firm Profitability,* Second Edition, by John G. Iezzi, ABA Law Practice Management Section, 2003.
- ◆ *The Essential Formbook: Comprehensive Management Tools for Lawyers, Volume III: Calendar and File Management/Law Firm Financial Analysis,* by Gary A. Munneke and Anthony E. Davis, ABA Law Practice Management Section, 2003.
- ◆ *Activity-Based Cost Management: Making It Work,* by Gary Cokins, The McGraw Hill Companies, 1996.
- ◆ *Activity-Based Costing: Making It Work for Small & Mid-Sized Companies,* by Douglas T. Hicks, John Wiley & Sons, 1999.
- ◆ *Activity-Based Management: A Comprehensive Implementation Guide,* by Edward Forrest, McGraw-Hill, 1996.

Outside guidance from a certified public accountant, experienced in professional service firms and cost accounting issues, should also be sought.

## Basic Approaches to Compensation

The compensation systems in use in law firms fall into three basic categories:

1. A *subjective,* performance-related system is one in which the firm—acting through an individual, a committee, or as a whole—reviews the

performance of each member, including whatever management information is available, and subjectively determines a relative value for each partner.

2. A *lockstep* (or equal-sharing) system is one in which partners from the same class are advanced together until they reach a full share interest in the firm. In its extreme form, this system eliminates the intermediate steps and all partners immediately share on an equal basis.

3. An *objective,* performance-related system attempts, through the use of various criteria, to arrive at a numeric value to determine compensation.

The preference of methods varies considerably by firm size. Overall, a combination system is most preferred, followed by objective and subjective approaches. A lockstep system as the sole system, or in combination with another philosophy, is least preferred in the U.S.

## Subjective Compensation Systems

One might think that small law firms would tend to be more subjectively oriented. They have the advantage of daily contact among the partners, which tends to make ongoing evaluation and intimate knowledge of everyone's contributions easier to achieve. Extending that logic, one would expect larger law firms to lean toward more formulaic approaches, due to the lack of daily interaction among partners. A study, however, found that more than 40 percent of law firms with one hundred or more lawyers, and less than 25 percent of firms with fewer than twenty lawyers, relied solely on subjective criteria for compensation decisions.[9]

A subjective compensation system embodies the concept of rough justice or acceptability—a system of relative compensation that one intuitively knows is balanced. Individual compensation decisions and overall compensation alignment are "right." The system is based on a sense of fair dealing.

## Percentages and Points

Traditionally, when lawyers establish new law partnerships, interests are distributed as percentages. The total of all interests must always add up to 100 percent. Percentages suffer from a psychological impairment, as one can advance only at the expense of someone else (a zero-sum game). For example, let's say that three individuals start a law partnership with each agreeing to share equally in the profits and losses and each contributing equally to the capital. After a few years, they add a fourth partner to the firm. The fourth partner is to share in 15 percent of the profits or losses and contributes 15 percent of the capital. This leaves each of the three founders with a 28.33 percent interest in the firm. Each capital account must be adjusted to bring the entire system into balance. As the three founders reach the peak of their careers, they are proud of the firm's growth, which they attribute primarily to their skills. However, they are concerned that their ownership and profit-sharing interests continue to dilute with the advancement of each new partner. In addition, many of their junior partners annually grouse at their percentage level. The eventual result is that no one is willing to give up percentages.

This is a common scenario. It makes little difference to the participants that they make more and more money each year. This is because they have increased the value of their interests faster than the dilution impact of growth. Now let's consider an economy in decline (such as the early 1990s or mid-2000 to early 2003). The firm's key specialty practice collapses. Incomes fall as costs continue to rise and business in other areas remains stagnant. The founders push to maintain their positions and junior partners push to regain lost income. Their only tool is to reallocate the partnership interests, which must still total 100 percent. This is extremely difficult without a pool of retiring or withdrawing partners from whom percentages may be recaptured.

Many firms in this situation change to a point system. Rather than artificially remaining at 100 points regardless of firm size, and reallocating points as new partners are admitted or as junior partners advance, the firm now assigns points on the basis of criteria developed to facilitate a rational compensation relationship among all the partners. Total points are not limited to 100. Frequently, this alleviates anxiety surrounding the individual giving and receiving of points. Of course, there is no real difference between percentages and points. The income pie remains the same.

A critical consideration in partner and shareholder compensation is the relation of compensation of one owner to another, in addition to the income of the firm as a whole. The first question is "what is the desired pay relationship between a newly admitted partner and the most highly paid partner in the firm?" The multiple from lowest to highest can be as little as 1.0 to 1.5, and is frequently 5.0 or higher, depending on the size of the firm; the age, experience, and seniority distributions within the firm; the amount of profits; the relative control of the firm's book of business; the type of practice; and the aggressiveness of the partners. Larger firms tend to have higher ratios than smaller firms, and insurance defense firms tend to have lower ratios than firms with a corporate practice, according to data from the Altman Weil annual *Survey of Law Firm Economics.*[10]

If a low-to-high ratio of, for example, 1:4 is desired, one could initiate a point system in which the most highly paid partner receives a maximum of 100 points, and the most junior partner a minimum of 25 points. To ascertain the value of each point, one need only divide the total number of points issued into the sum available for distribution.

The point spread used should significantly differentiate between one number and the next. For higher-paid partners who earn large sums of money, a distinction of a few hundred or even a few thousand dollars in compensation per year may be important psychologically, but it is meaningless in economic terms. For lower-paid partners, there is the continuing question, "How can the compensation system be so precise that it can differentiate by so small a sum?" Law firms have lost productive individuals over such matters, leading to significant morale problems.

In determining the number of points to be used, a firm should consider what significant differentiations it wants. One can achieve a 1:4 ratio by using a minimum of 5 points and a maximum of 20 points, just as well as by using a maximum of 100 or 1,000. For individuals between the maximum and minimum of the 5:20 system, 1 additional point should provide a significant change in earnings. For the 100 or 1,000 systems, a 1-point difference produces a markedly smaller change in compensation.

Point systems are easier to administer than percentage systems, but they are a version of the same method of compensation. Lockstep or equal-sharing systems can also use percentages or points in quantifying the allocation of profits.

## How Subjective Compensation Systems Work

How do subjective compensation—or rough justice—systems work? Some firms approach them in a democratic manner. For example, each partner is asked to participate in the process, perhaps through a questionnaire or verbal comments during the income distribution meeting. One or more members of a compensation committee may interview partners. Ballots or scorecards may be used, whereby partners provide judgments on other partners' performance in specific areas. Smaller law firms can effectively handle these deliberations in a single meeting and often without rancor. Larger firms may need several months to gather the information and allow the participation process to work.

Some firms use a committee to perform the evaluation (absent formal participation of each partner). In practice, such a committee typically tests the water to ensure that its general thinking is in keeping with that of the firm. Compensation committee reports that contain surprises require significantly more selling to get approved.

When ballots or scorecards are used, the firm is actually quantifying subjective factors to provide some methodical way to make compensation decisions. Below is a ballot using scoring techniques that a firm may wish to consider if its current process is not working as well as desired. Most scoring systems provide for additional adjustments after scoring, to avoid inappropriate results.

*Ballot.*    A ballot system develops rankings by scoring each partner's performance in enumerated areas. Ballots are usually secret. Scoring is often on a scale of one to ten (but any scale will work).

| Basic Scorecard for Partner Able (Scale 1–10) | | | | | | | | | | | |
|---|---|---|---|---|---|---|---|---|---|---|---|
| Criteria ↓ | Ratings Partners ⟶ | | | | | | | | Total | Ballot | Olympic |
| | $P_1$ | $P_2$ | $P_3$ | $P_4$ | $P_5$ | $P_6$ | $P_7$ | (Etc.) | | | |
| Productivity | 8 | 6 | 8 | ⑨ | 7 | ⑤ | 8 | | 51 | 7.3 | 7.4 |
| Market Visibility | 7 | ⑤ | 6 | ⑨ | 7 | 6 | 8 | | 48 | 6.9 | 6.8 |
| Management | ④ | 4 | 5 | 6 | ⑦ | 5 | 5 | | 36 | 5.7 | 5.0 |
| Policy Adherence | 7 | ⑧ | 8 | ③ | 7 | 5 | 8 | | 46 | 6.6 | 7.0 |
| Technical Skill | 8 | 7 | ⑨ | 8 | 7 | ⑥ | 8 | | 53 | 7.6 | 7.6 |
| Client Satisfaction | 9 | 9 | ⑩ | 10 | ⑦ | 8 | 8 | | 61 | 8.7 | 8.8 |
| Etc. | | | | | | | | | | | |

Note: circled ratings are low and high for each criteria and are excluded for Olympic scoring.

*Olympic scoring system.*    This is a ballot approach that rejects the highest and lowest scores and averages the remaining scores. This system helps offset the problem of outliers. Determining the median value instead of an average also works, but is more difficult to calculate.

*Point accumulation.*    This is a scorecard system that allows each attribute to have different maximum point values. For example, quality of work may have a maximum of 25 points, training and development of associates may have a maximum of 10 points, business development may have a maximum of 20 points, and so on. This system offers great flexibility, as a firm can change the relative importance of factors as the needs of the firm change.

Point accumulation can also be used to design individual strength-based compensation systems. For example, the firm determines that there are ten performance areas critical to its success. Each partner is reviewed to determine which performance areas represent that partner's strengths. The firm also decides that each partner will have the opportunity to earn a total of 50 compensation points. At the start of each year the firm and the partner agree on which performance areas represent that partner's strengths and the allocation of points among those areas. Generally, each partner will have three to six out of the ten total performance areas to which the 50 points are allocated. At the end of the year there is a performance assessment of the partner in each of the agreed-upon performance areas and a grade is assigned to each performance area. The grade and the point allocation are combined to determine how many total points that partner earned for the year.

*Direct assignment.* With this approach, the partners or committee members are asked to determine each partner's compensation. This method is usually implemented in one of three ways:

a. The scorecards ask for a dollar figure for each partner; the total must equal distributable income.
b. The scorecards ask for a percentage; the total must equal 100 percent.
c. Each partner is assigned a point value that may not exceed a certain amount (say 50 points); the total points awarded for a given partner will usually vary from one scorecard to another.

## Applying Compensation Criteria

Apportioning profit is a complex and difficult task. There are no right or wrong answers. Partner compensation is more art than science. Rough justice requires evaluation of the individual, comparing the evaluation against those of all other partners, and relating the determinations to available funds. In this part of the process of setting compensation, the concepts of risk sharing, permitted disparity, and peer group are very important. Each firm will have a different sense of what should be done in these areas.

*Risk sharing.* How much risk should a junior partner be asked to assume? How does that compare with midlevel and senior partners? In addition, if one's risk is limited, should one's reward be limited as well? If yes, would that still be true in high-profit years? These questions need consideration in a subjective compensation system.

*Permitted disparity.* Altman Weil was once asked the question, "Is the individual making $100,000 truly a partner with the individual making $1 million?" It's an interesting question to consider. At what point does the disparity between the highest-paid partner and lowest-paid partner become so vast that the concept of partnership breaks down? Are there exceptions? Does it really matter? The answers vary. Generally, in firms of fewer than one hundred lawyers, once the ratio of the highest-paid to lowest-paid partner exceeds 6:1, there is a loss of partnership identity. Larger firms seem more comfortable with spreads in excess of 6:1; their size and operating economics allow for such differences. Often, if you go beyond the one or two highest-paid partners, the ratio for the balance of the partners becomes much closer. This is a typical pattern in a law firm with one or two superstar rainmakers.

***Peer group.***    Those who recognize the imperfection of the compensation process often believe that it is inappropriate to have small differences in compensation for partners who have small differences in performance. More havoc has been wrought with compensation differences of only a few thousand dollars than one would ever believe possible! The peer group concept is a means to resolve that situation. Individuals with similar overall evaluations are grouped together and all are assigned the same compensation. Compensation gaps between different peer groups are usually significant ($20,000 or more). This strategy is designed to head off second-guessing about small differences in compensation.

As stated earlier, rough-justice factors should change over time as a firm's needs change. They can also change for a single individual over time. As an example, a junior partner, who feels terribly underpaid at $125,000 while generating $250,000 in personal fee receipts and having no book of business, may develop a far different view several years later when he or she is controlling $600,000 in business and generating $300,000 in fee receipts. Then it no longer seems fair to subsidize junior partners who have no books of business; the more senior partners must be paid for their books of business and the work they perform.

In addition, a junior partner with a family, mortgage, schooling, orthodontics, and no savings may feel far less generous about compensation apportionment—he or she is trying to meet everyday obligations and live the lifestyle appropriate for his or her position—than does the senior partner who is more secure and has fewer financial obligations. Each of these individuals will approach the compensation decision differently. Naturally, each is approaching it from his or her own economic situation.

These different positions are often very difficult to reconcile. To start, one must first develop an understanding of each partner's expectations regarding compensation. One then must find or create some common ground from which a workable system can be fashioned. Often, the assistance of an impartial individual is required—one who can hear all sides, summarize the issues, and direct the partners toward common ground.

Using rough justice is a subjective approach to compensation that, admittedly, requires more effort to implement than does an objective (formulaic) system. For many law firms, however, it is the best way to achieve a perception of fairness and to encourage partners to behave in ways that will lead to the success of the firm as a whole.

## Lockstep or Equal-Sharing Systems

Historically a prominent compensation method, the lockstep approach is now the least preferred way of allocating compensation in the U.S. However, in the U.K., lockstep still dominates. In the U.S., it is perceived to be out of step with the economic consequences of a maturing legal marketplace. As the post–World War II lawyers approach retirement, more and more of them expect to be paid for their contributions on a current basis and are much less willing to carry a partner (sometimes even for only a short period of time) whose productivity slips. However, as with any compensation system, there are advantages and disadvantages to the lockstep method. Partners should have candid discussions about all systems to determine which compensation tenets fit their personalities and relationships.

Some law firms develop a profit-distribution system under which partners are given specific income units on admission, and advanced a number of units each year until they reach a determined maximum. For example, a few partners may receive four units on admission, and one additional unit per year, until a maximum of ten units is achieved. In a firm like this, it takes six years from partnership admission to become a full partner.

Such a system is entirely noncompetitive. It requires only that each partner make an appropriate contribution according to his or her ability, and each is rewarded equally. On the other hand, the system is totally lacking in accountability. Once a partner is admitted, progress becomes automatic and no reduction in income share is ever experienced. Such a lack of accountability favors the least energetic, least aggressive, and least capable lawyers. It does little to reward hard work, sales ability, or expertise. In such a system, some partners retire at their desks long before formal retirement, and yet continue to receive a full share.

This type of system can be discouraging to the most energetic partners and to those seeking higher incomes. These partners are discouraged by the small impact their individual efforts have on the overall profit of the firm. This inability to affect their own earnings in any substantial way can eventually lead to a considerable level of frustration, and loss of some exceptional partners.

A number of refinements can be made to a lockstep system, which would improve its acceptability and preserve its major strengths—simplicity, lack of confrontation, and lack of internal competition (scorekeeping).

Lawyers' compensation, as previously indicated, typically rises until around the thirtieth year of practice, and then tends to plateau or slightly decrease until lawyers begin to retire. The relatively short period during which lawyers in the hypothetical firm reach parity means that the firm's practices are out of step with the statistical profile of the profession. One refinement would be to lengthen the time for equal sharing to twenty years of practice. In the process, the number of points used is increased. An advancement schedule could be established that allows more rapid advancement in the first two years, and then a slowing until a full share is reached.

For a lockstep system to work, the firm must do two things. First, it must adopt standards of performance (a comfort-zone concept developed by Altman Weil is an appropriate approach). Second, the firm must apply the standards and have zero tolerance for chronic underperformance. In this way, the system's weaknesses are mitigated.

Firm standards should include a specific budget for firm time for those partners with managerial or committee assignments. Authorized management time may be credited, wholly or in part, toward time budgets. When an individual accepts a leadership position in a community enterprise, such as a bar presidency or the head of a fund drive, and when the firm approves the activity in advance, a time budget could be established and made part of the quota. Individual partners who consistently fail to achieve the budgeted hours might have their units of participation reduced, until their effort and shares of profit come into balance. Only disability or the expressed advance action of the firm might excuse a partner from meeting budgeted hours.

In addition to establishing accountability for the performance of a certain amount of professional work, an incentive or bonus program can operate in conjunction with a lockstep distribution system. Recognition of good work is an important stimulant to productivity and can be used successfully by a law firm.

To provide incentive, the firm might budget an annual fund to be allocated by its policy committee during the last month of the year. The amounts awarded could be specified, say, as no less than $20,000 for partners and the firm administrator, and $10,000 for associates and other exempt support staff. The initial size of the fund might be 5 percent of gross fees collected during the year. The committee may not be required to distribute any or all of the money set aside for this purpose. Minimum award sizes require that the policy committee not simply spread the available funds among all the partners. The addition of an incentive plan to a lockstep compensation system enables the firm to provide meaningful recognition to those partners whose efforts achieve a special result for the firm. Bonuses reward extraordinary contributions, and therefore differ from profit sharing. (Profit sharing relates to the distribution of financial success among all owners in some predetermined manner, but not based on a single year's contribution.)

Another incentive is to permit disparity of plus or minus some percentage (say 10 percent) around the lockstep target. The lockstep range is then administered by the firm, its management, or a special committee. It is possible to mix additional formulaic criteria or rely on subjective determination to position individuals within the appropriate range.

### *Objective Distribution Systems*
### "Hale & Dorr System" of Reginald Heber Smith

Formula distribution systems were first made popular by the writings of the late Reginald Heber Smith, who was then the managing partner of Hale & Dorr in Boston. These distribution systems are still popular today. To set the stage for discussion, we quote from the pamphlet *Law Office Organization* by Smith, published by the ABA in 1943[11] (the material first appeared in the *American Bar Association Journal* in 1940):

> Every partner has a percentage or share of profits; those shares must total 100 percent. If a partner is entitled to be increased by 1 percent, some other partners must be decreased by 1 percent and that is where the rub comes. This is best overcome through records that are impersonal, but which indicate plainly what adjustments among partners are in order.
>
> It has been our experience over a number of years that all such adjustments can be made in good spirit and without rancor, in a very brief space of time, and by unanimous vote of all partners provided thorough and painstaking work has been done in advance by the manager (the managing partner).
>
> All the records that show what every partner has done exist. They need only to be assembled. At the end of the fiscal year four facts about each partner are known:
>
> 1. What he has received from the firm (his drawing allowance plus his share of profits for the fiscal year).
> 2. What he has contributed to the firm through work (this is the total of his "prorated" earnings plus any time charged to the firm).
> 3. What he has contributed to the firm through business brought in (this is the total of bills sent out during the fiscal year in cases in which he was responsible lawyer, less any bills that went to "bad" during the fiscal year).
> 4. What he has contributed to the firm through the profit on such business (this is the excess of bill over cost, less the loss when cost exceeds bill or the bill has gone to "bad" during the fiscal year).

Just as partners' shares in profits are expressed in percentages, so these figures must be converted into percentages.

This can be illustrated by assuming a firm with four partners, using round figures, and we will do the sum for Item 2—Work Done.

| *Partner* | *Value of Work Done* | *Percent* |
|---|---|---|
| A | $20,000 | 50.00% |
| B | 10,000 | 25.00 |
| C | 7,500 | 18.75 |
| D | 2,500 | 6.25 |
| | $40,000 | 100.00% |

Exactly the same thing is done for business credit and profit credit. Again, this will be illustrated by using the same four partners.

| *Partner* | *Business Credit* | | *Profit Center* | |
|---|---|---|---|---|
| | *Amount* | *Percent* | *Amount* | *Percent* |
| A | $20,000 | 40% | $ 4,000 | 40% |
| B | 15,000 | 30 | 2,000 | 20 |
| C | 10,000 | 20 | 3,000 | 30 |
| D | 5,000 | 10 | 1,000 | 10 |
| | $50,000 | 100% | $10,000 | 100% |

We think these three different kinds of contribution by a partner to the firm are not of equal importance. We think work done is most important, business credit next, and profit credit last. To reflect the different degrees of importance we "weight" the percentages. (Any firm is entitled to come to its own decision about this and to use any weighting it likes.) Work done is weighted at 6 (multiplied by 6), business credit is weighted at 3, and profit credit at 1. The total is divided by 10. The result is still a percentage figure and that figure we call "Value Produced." The following table shows the mathematics.

| | *Work Done* | | *Business Credit* | | *Profit Center* | | | *Divided by 10 Gives Value Produced* |
|---|---|---|---|---|---|---|---|---|
| *1* | *2* | *3* | *4* | *5* | *6* | *7* | | |
| *Partner* | *%* | *x6* | *%* | *x3* | *%* | *x1* | *3 + 5 + 7* | |
| A | 50.00 | 300.0 | 40 | 120 | 40 | 40 | 460.0 | 46.00 |
| B | 25.00 | 150.0 | 30 | 90 | 20 | 20 | 260.0 | 26.00 |
| C | 18.75 | 112.5 | 20 | 60 | 30 | 30 | 202.5 | 20.25 |
| D | 6.25 | 37.5 | 10 | 30 | 10 | 10 | 77.5 | 7.75 |
| | 100.0% | 600.0 | 100% | 300 | 100% | 100 | 1,000.0 | 100.00 |

What each partner has received from the firm is reduced to a percentage and that figure is called "Value Received." Let us also make that computation:

| Partner | Received from the Firm | |
|---|---|---|
| | *Amount* | *Percent* |
| A | $10,000 | 40% |
| B | 6,000 | 24 |
| C | 5,000 | 20 |
| D | 4,000 | 16 |
| | $25,000 | 100% |

The manager's report will end up with two final figures for each partner—i.e., "Value Produced" and "Value Received." Statistically, each partner has produced more than he has received or has received more than he has produced. In the former case he has a credit and in the latter case a deficit. We can now state these final figures:

| Partner | Value Produced | Received from Firm | Credit | Deficit |
|---|---|---|---|---|
| A | 46.00% | 40.00% | +6.00 | |
| B | 26.00 | 24.00 | +2.00 | |
| C | 20.25 | 20.00 | +0.25 | |
| D | 7.75 | 16.00 | | −8.25 |
| | 100.00% | 100.00% | +8.25 | −8.25 |

There are ups and downs in law practice so that a one-year record is too short a time on which to base a judgment. Hence, exactly the same figures are made up in cumulative form and embracing all years for which we have these records.

These two tables (one giving the annual and the other the cumulative figures) are typed and a copy goes to every partner. He thus has the whole story and he has exactly the same evidential material as has the manager. The manager writes and sends to each partner a short report suggesting that one or more partners have their shares in profits increased and others accept decreases. The partners meet and customarily the report is accepted without debate. That fixes the share in profits of each partner for the next fiscal year. Having gotten over the tough part the partners then relax and enjoy a squabble over whether the youngest junior (i.e., associate) shall have any raise in pay and if so, how much.

As to juniors, the manager prepares somewhat similar tables, but they are simpler. Figures about juniors need not be converted into percentages and there need be no weighting. The record sets out what each junior has earned by work done (measured by prorating), business credit, profit on such business, hours worked, value of hours produced (hours worked multiplied by cost per hour) and present salary.

It can readily be argued that all the qualities and values of a lawyer cannot be caught in a statistical net no matter how finely spun. That allegation is conceded. But the question is: "What better method is there?"

It is impersonal, it is open and aboveboard, it does yield a vast amount of information, and it has been assembled in the manner which the partners themselves have decided to be as fair as they can make it and which they have incorporated into their partnership articles. After prescribing the method, the partnership articles do not say that the statistical tabulations are conclusive, but that they shall be considered "as substantial evidence."

The figures are not given literal application. If a partner has a credit (excess of value produced over value received) of 2 points, that does not mean that he shall at once have his share of profits increased 2 points. But if, year by year, the partner has been maintaining a credit, it is evident that he should have some increase.

Furthermore, anyone who deals with such figures is bound to be impressed by the fact that while the figures for one year are an adequate base, the cumulative figures as they are kept year after year grow progressively more accurate until they do approximate the truth and afford an adequate basis for judgment by a group of partners whose intention and desire is to deal justly with one another.

With their internal affairs settled, the partners can depart on vacation. . . .

Although Smith collected data, he and his firm did not directly apply the information to compensation. That, however, is the course some law firms adopted. If compensation is to be determined on the basis of value of work done, business credit, and profit credit, then consideration must also be given to the other factors that are compensable—those factors that are listed earlier in this chapter. In particular, credit must be allocated for management of the firm and for training associates and staff, or these functions will be neglected.

Implementation of a formula-based income distribution system may make it difficult to maintain specialties in a firm. Areas of law that are perceived to be lucrative—in that they pay more than the base hourly rate—will be sought by all lawyers, regardless of their training. Service areas, such as estate planning and some aspects of tax work, might be avoided if they pay at less than standard value.

The allocation of credit for business obtained can be a difficult process. When a firm obtains a new client, the allocation decision is usually easy because it is clear who is responsible for the firm receiving the client's work. But when client A sends client B to an individual who is not the originator of client A, a problem arises. Also, when a client has been in a firm for a good number of years and has been served by many of the firm's lawyers, there is a question about the allocation of credit. Obviously, unless all the lawyers have served the client well, the client might be long gone from the firm. This raises a question of how long sales credit should be allocated to the originating lawyer. Some firms have resolved this issue by giving a less highly weighted credit for client maintenance once the client is established within the firm—for example, after a period of three to five years.

There are other problems in assigning origination credits. Some clients come to a firm because of its general reputation, not because of a specific lawyer. How will such clients be credited? Will credit go to the lawyers who happened to be called by the receptionist, or will there be a firm or department credit?

To a considerable degree, credits for bringing in clients, and, to some degree, production credits, can be manipulated. In some firms, it is not unusual to find credit in the partner production column for work actually performed by a secretary or legal assistant (and occasionally by an associate). An associate's time might later be written off as training, while the supervising partner gets full work credit.

Credit systems of every sort may skew lawyers' behavior, just as tax laws may skew economic behavior. And, as with tax laws, not all the resultant behavior can be anticipated when a plan is adopted, nor is all the behavior beneficial.

Profitability can be measured by comparing the fee with the value of time at standard rates, but this can be distorted when inexperienced personnel are assigned to a case and their time is then written off. On the other hand, care must be taken not to penalize the responsible lawyer just because he or she has agreed to use a case for training a fledgling lawyer or paralegal.

Law firms that wish to allocate credit for business obtained generally develop an extensive set of rules for crediting the function. Such rules may provide for division of origination credit between two or more partners claiming the credit, and may set limits on the time frame over which the credit is awarded.

A set of rules is also required for the crediting value of work done when more than one lawyer is involved in producing the fee. The basic fee structure of most law firms recognizes that lawyers are not of equal value. Table 1.2 shows the relationship between hourly rates and years of experience, based on the first admission to practice law.

Based on this data, a lawyer with under two years of experience would need nearly two hours of work to obtain the same value that a lawyer with 21 or more years of experience receives for one hour of work. When fees are not charged at the standard value, the difference must be allocated. In many firms this allocation is done pro rata, as shown in Table 1.3.

**TABLE 1.2**
**Standard Hourly Billing Rate by Years of Legal Experience,**
**as of January 1, 2003**

| Years of Experience | Average | Median |
|---|---|---|
| Under 2 years | $149 | $145 |
| 2–3 years | 167 | 160 |
| 4–5 years | 185 | 175 |
| 6–7 years | 198 | 190 |
| 8–10 years | 214 | 200 |
| 11–15 years | 227 | 225 |
| 16–20 years | 250 | 240 |
| 21 or more years | 270 | 260 |

Source: *SURVEY OF LAW FIRM ECONOMICS* (Newtown Square, PA: Altman Weil Publications, Inc., 2003), 115.

**TABLE 1.3**
**A Method for Dividing Credit for Doing Work, Based on Time Records and**
**Standard Hourly Rates (*partner's standard hourly rate is $270; associate's***
***standard hourly rate is $150*)**

| Lawyer | Hours Recorded | × | Hourly Rate | = | Time/Dollar Value | = | % of Total |
|---|---|---|---|---|---|---|---|
| Partner | 3 | × | $270 | = | $ 810 | = | 64.3% |
| Associate | 3 | × | $150 | = | $ 450 | = | 35.7% |
| Total | | | | | $1,260 | | 100.0% |

If the actual fee collected is $1,000, credit the partner with 64.3% ($643), and credit the associate with 35.7 percent ($357). If the fee collected is $1,500, credit the partner with $964, and credit the associate with $536.

In some firms, the assisting lawyers and paralegals are credited at standard hourly rates, and the responsible or billing lawyer gets whatever is left. In other firms, billing partners are given full discretion in allocating credits on their matters.

In the system described by Smith, weighting factors are given as 6, 3, and 1, but it is noted that other firms may weight the three factors differently. Giving only twice as much weight to producing work as to obtaining it places a high value on the sales function. Firms with an established clientele may want to place greater emphasis on getting the work done. Firms in a start-up situation, or firms with a desire to expand or with a predominantly transactional practice may, on the other hand, give greater weight to producing clients. Once a system of weights is established, however, it is difficult to change. Some individuals will fall into the role of producing work, while others will excel in obtaining clients. When a change in weighting is proposed, somebody's ox is gored and, consequently, change is resisted. This means that the firm's incentive system may not be aligned with the firm's real needs.

One year doesn't make a career, and the numbers produced in one year should not alone determine compensation for the following year, as Smith notes. Few firms, however, want to be burdened by the accumulation of data for the whole history of the organization. Many firms use a moving average of three, four, or five years when they employ formula measures.

As can be gathered from the foregoing, formula compensation systems can become quite complicated and expensive. Appendix 1 is an example of the complexity of one law firm's formula plan.

## Work-Purchase Systems

Some law firms use an alternative credit system. It is sometimes referred to as the work-purchase system. In this approach, the lawyer who obtains a client is regarded as the manager of that client's work. The lawyer may call upon the services of any part of the firm, and is expected to use those people most capable of handling the client's problem at the lowest price. An obtaining lawyer who does not want to handle the legal work for which he or she is approached may find another lawyer in the firm who wants to manage the matter. In this case, the obtaining lawyer turns over total responsibility and all credit to the other lawyer.

Each lawyer and paralegal is assigned a standard billing rate for each year. The manager of a file, at his or her discretion, buys time from other lawyers and paralegals at a percentage (such as 85 percent) of the producing lawyer's and paralegal's standard rate. The manager is then free to set a billing rate for the client at any rate above or below the standard rate, depending on all the billing factors. Contingent-fee work is also charged to its manager at a percentage of the standard rate. All lawyers and paralegals keep time records on a client-by-client and case-by-case basis.

Each partner who has managerial responsibility for the firm is assigned a budget of hours for management activities, including the training of associates and paralegals. The system credits lawyers for such activities at a percentage of standard hourly rates.

Retainers paid in advance are credited to the account of a responsible partner when received, and debited when funds are reallocated to other lawyers who have performed services. Figures are accumulated for all producing personnel, including associate lawyers and paralegal assistants. Partner-managers do not get the free use of income-producing personnel of the firm. When a matter is completed, or at the end of each year, the account of the responsible lawyer is adjusted to deduct all credits allocated to other lawyers and legal assistants.

If the manager of a case expends more professional effort than the fee justifies, he or she may end up with a loss, resulting in a reduction from accumulated credits. If, on the other hand, the matter is billed at more than standard fees, there may be a large excess (premium) of credit over and above the percentage called for by the discounted standard rate. In most firms, associate lawyers are not permitted to be billing lawyers, and, consequently, are limited to providing services at a percentage of the standard rate.

This system encourages use of efficient people and specialized talent. It offers ample reward for the individual who has the ability to obtain clients, without giving that person any incentive to perform the most highly paid work and farm out the lesser-paid activities.

The work-purchase system does not encourage training or other administrative and managerial activities because such activities reflect only a discounted rate value. In addition, partners lose the ability to generate leveraged profits and the potential for premiums from billable work if time is invested in discounted firm activities. Also, the system concentrates much of the firm's work on a few good people, and could adversely affect the morale and economic health of the firm as a whole. It may restrict access to the firm's resources by junior partners or others without sufficient clout.

## Tiered Systems

Some firms allocate a base dollar amount for each owner. It may be called a draw or a salary. If there are funds available for distribution after all base amounts are paid, such funds are usually not distributed in accord with the relationship of base amounts to each other. At one extreme, for example, funds available for distribution may be allocated equally among the partners. That type of system will provide a considerable incentive for all partners to ensure the firm's profits. Generically, these systems are referred to as "tiered" compensation systems.

Sometimes there are various pools of funds available for distribution. For example, if base compensation uses the first $500,000 of distributable funds, the next $100,000 might be shared equally, and amounts above that—or above $600,000—might be distributed in some other way. The final pool may be distributed on the basis of production, peer evaluation, a determined point or percentage interest, or many other factors. Tiering of this type enables a law firm to provide various incentives.

Sometimes there are specified requirements for receipt of amounts above the base draw or salary. Such requirements may be based on billing a certain number of hours, obtaining business, or meeting other predetermined objectives. In other situations, tiers are used to provide junior partners with greater interest in the firm's profits, beyond the current base.

The following section ("Can a Partner's Value Be Measured?") discusses a more sophisticated analysis than many firms may wish to undergo. A simplified version of the formula, using the same definitions as discussed below, is a quick tool to assess the market value of a partner. The likely market range of compensation for an individual is –10% of *P* to +20% of *P*. The si mula is $P = (C_w - O) + M_a(C_r - C_w)$.

# Can a Partner's Value Be Measured?

Yes. It is done all the time. More precisely, the question is "can we use a mathematical formula to reliably determine the value of a partner, such that it is both internally and externally rational?" Again, the answer is yes, but subject to the culture and values of the organization. The following formula has been used for several years by a variety of firms in a variety of settings. With an acknowledged relevant range around the formula's answer, it has been a successful tool.

## *The Basic Formula*

Years of consideration of this issue have led Altman Weil to the conclusion that the fundamental formula is:

$P = Ma(Cr - Cw) + Rp(Cw + Vf) - O$
where:
$P$ = individual partner's economic value
$Ma$ = margin on associates
$Cr$ = responsible-lawyer credits of the individual partner
$Cw$ = working-lawyer credits of the individual partner
$Rp$ = firmwide realization on partner revenues
$Vf$ = value of individual partner time expended in firm-authorized efforts, at standard rates
$O$ = per-lawyer overhead

In effect, the formula states that a partner's economic value is measured by the economic value of revenues generated by his or her individual efforts on behalf of clients, plus profits generated by associates on matters managed by the partner, minus the partner's individually allocated overhead. All credits in the formula (*C* factors) are measured on the basis of fees received. Time worked is irrelevant if not revenue generating, unless the firm itself is willing to pay for it out of revenues that otherwise would be shared by those partners who generated them. *O* factors are also calculated on a cash basis.

## Margin on Associates (Ma)

Margin on associates (*Ma*) refers to profit on work done by associates, calculated on a cash receipts basis. Paralegals can be included in the margin calculation if desired, which means their compensation is removed from overhead for purposes of computing margin. If paralegals are not included, they are treated as part of overhead. Not including them simply increases both responsible-lawyer credits and working-lawyer credits, as well as per-lawyer overhead.

$Ma$ is the sum of associate working-lawyer credits on fees received, minus their combined compensation and allocated overhead, as a percentage of their combined revenues. Overhead for these purposes may be computed firm-wide on a per-lawyer basis; if paralegals are included, separately for lawyers and paralegals; if substantially different for partners and associates, separately for each; or even individually calculated for specific groups of lawyers (in a particular department, for example) or for each individual associate and paralegal, if necessary. In effect:

$$Ma = [\Sigma\, Cwa - Sa - (Oa \times A)] / \Sigma\, Cwa$$

where:

$\Sigma\, Cwa$ = aggregate associate working credits

$Sa$ = associate salaries and benefits

$Oa$ = per-associate overhead

$A$ = number of associates

## Responsible-Lawyer Credits (Cr)

Responsible-lawyer credits ($Cr$) are the combined effect of both originating and managing-billing partners. If a firm tracks origination, $Cr$ is the full value of all matters both originated and managed (billed) by the partner, one-half the value of matters originated by that partner but managed and billed by another, and one-half the value of matters originated by others but managed and billed by him or her. If the firm does not track origination, $Cr$ is simply the value of billing-partner credits, measured on a receipts basis.

The formula assumes that origination and management of legal matters are equally important. In today's environment, that is probably a fair evaluation. However, if necessary, a different relationship can be incorporated into the formula.

## Working-Lawyer Credits (Cw)

Working-lawyer credits ($Cw$) of individual partners also are measured on a cash receipts basis. This concept is employed in most law firms, but can be controversial, depending upon how allocation of fees is made on multiple-lawyer matters. This can be done:

a. At the discretion of the billing lawyer (in which case, most discounts will result in writing off all associate time, while maintaining the full value of partner time)

b. On a prorated basis, whereby the computer automatically calculates the discount to be applied to the value of each lawyer's work, whether partner or associate, based on relative time values

c. By first crediting associate time at standard rates, and allowing partners to assume credit for whatever balance remains, be it a discount from standard rates, or a premium

Regardless of which method is used, it must be applied consistently within the firm. Otherwise, *Cw* is going to mean very different things for different partners.

## Realization on Partner Revenues (Rp)

The concept of realization on partner revenues (*Rp*) is the key to operation of the formula. It takes into account the value of firm time (authorized and for which partners are accountable) for both management and marketing functions—including recruitment, associate training, business management, practice management, firm marketing (other than individual rainmaking), pro bono work, and the like—at each partner's billing rate. It assumes the firm's ability to delegate, provide authority, specialize, and require accountability for these functions. It is not applicable to things all partners are expected to do, or to certain functions that are equally spread among all partners. The concept considers the fact that if specific, identified partners did not, for example, manage the firm or its departments, others would have to do it, and, therefore, the economic-opportunity cost of self-management must be spread among all. This factor reduces the economic value of revenues attributable to each partner's work (working-lawyer credits) by the economic-opportunity cost of otherwise billable hours spread through the firm. The *Rp* factor is essentially the summation of working-lawyer credits divided by those credits plus the economic value of authorized firm credits, at standard rates. In effect:

$$Rp = \Sigma \, Cw \, / \, (\Sigma \, Cw + \Sigma \, Vf)$$
where:
$\Sigma \, Cw$ = aggregate partner working credits
$\Sigma \, Vf$ = aggregate authorized firm credits

## Overhead (O)

The last factor, overhead (*O*), can be computed on a per-lawyer basis for the firm as a whole. If there is a substantial difference between overhead allocation to partners and associates, it can be computed separately for each, and used on that basis in the different components of the formula. Remember, paralegals should not be included in overhead if they are treated separately in the *Ma* calculation.

## *Assumptions*

The basic formula to determine a partner's value includes the following key assumptions:

- Associate margins are substantially the same throughout the firm. If not, they can be computed separately for each department, or even for each associate.
- Paralegals can be considered associates for *Ma* computation, although in that case overhead for purposes of that computation may become "overhead per nonpartner fee earner."
- Firm time is credited in *Vf* only for official, individually assigned functions, such as managing partner, executive committee, business development committee, recruiting, training, departmental management, and the like. Time commitments of each will be different, and may be limited to a budget, in some cases.
- Overhead per partner is not substantially different from overhead per lawyer. If so, it can be computed separately for each.
- All matters are managed and billed by a partner.
- Origination and management of legal matters are equally important.

## *Countervailing Arguments*

The primary argument against determining a partner's economic value by formula is that the formula does not measure the value of seniority, bar and community activities, management or training contributions, teamwork, cooperation, and the like. These arguments are only partially apposite.

One could argue that seniority is irrelevant, as senior lawyers generally are charged at higher rates and arguably should be generating more business for others to do. In any event, consider which is more valuable: a senior lawyer who generates no business but is fully productive as a working lawyer, or a junior lawyer who generates well over a million dollars a year worth of business for himself and others to do.

Besides offering public-relations opportunities, bar and community activities are likewise questionably relevant, except when they generate new business or when the firm has authorized their expenditure and is willing to credit the participating lawyers for all or part of their time at standard hourly rates. After all, how important is it for a partner to be president of the state bar association if it generates no business for the firm? Some argue that it is only as important as one's partners believe it (or its market value) to be, in which case they could pay him or her for it, at standard rates. Or, they could at least credit the individual with the hours expended in achieving and maintaining the position, at standard rates, recognizing that not only might this result in economic value (and probably income) to that partner, but also in a reduction of the economic valuation of each hour's worth of dollars collected for client work done by the other partners in the firm, under the rationale that were it not done by one partner, the firm would ask another to do it.

The formula induces a new level of scrutiny to economic (and non-revenue-producing) activities pursued in a law firm environment.

### Uses of the Concept

The concept of a measurement of economic value of a partner might be used for a number of purposes, including the following:

- Evaluating an existing partner compensation system, to determine its economic validity
- Providing a basis for commencement (only) of compensation review, by a compensation committee
- Determining the value of a book of business being brought by a lateral partner
- Adjusting economic performance of individual partners to improve overall firm economic performance
- Identifying the need for improvement of associate margin or partner realization, and measuring the effects of such improvement on individual partner incomes

## Pure Grinders and Finders: The Theoretical Value of Service Providers and Rainmakers

Both activities—providing service and rainmaking—are important and necessary for a successful law practice, but neither alone can be considered the full measure of a partner's contribution to the firm. Let's focus on the two extremes—the pure grinder and the pure finder. Understanding the extremes yields insight into dealing with the more typical situation of those lawyers who do both.

### The Pure Grinder

The archetypal service partner—one who originates no business of his or her own—contributes to the profits of the firm through personal labors on behalf of others' clients. This partner might also contribute by delegating to, and supervising the work of, associates (which would add value), but this analysis assumes the contribution is solely that of a performer of legal work.

In any given year, a grinder's economic contribution is measured by the excess of cash collected for services, over and above cash compensation (including benefits and perks) and the administrative cost of supporting his or her efforts (that is, secretarial help, rent, occupancy, and so on). For example, consider a new partner (male, for ease of pronoun reference) with the following profile:

| Age | 33 years old |
|---|---|
| Billable hours | 1,800 per year |
| Hourly rate | $170 per hour |
| Administrative cost | $110,000 per year |
| Cash compensation | $150,000 per year |
| | (cash plus benefits plus pension) |

If one assumes that the firm can bill and collect 95 percent of the value of his billable hours, and that the hours are all billed and collected in the same year, the partner's economic contribution to the firm in his first year is as follows:

| Hours | 1,800 |
|---|---|
| × Rate | × $170 |
| × Realization | × 95% |
| = Revenue | $290,700 |
| – Administrative Cost | –110,000 |
| – Compensation | –150,000 |
| = Contribution | $ 30,700 |

In essence, this hypothetical partner has generated sufficient revenue to cover his support costs, pay his compensation, and still leave $30,700 on the table for others to share. On the surface, one might easily conclude that this partner is probably undercompensated by as much as the amount of his excess contribution. Yet, to evaluate the partner's contribution properly, one must look beyond the results in the first year.

In any single year, it is conceivable that a pure service partner might generate remarkable numbers. But partnership is a long-term commitment and compensation systems must take into account economic contribution over the long term, not simply in any single year. (The only exception to this rule is the firm that operates on an "eat-what-you-kill" profit center compensation system; one that is probably better regarded as an office-sharing arrangement rather than a law firm in the true sense.) There will be some years in which the partner contributes excess value and others in which the firm will carry him. One hopes that over the course of a partner's career, the excess dollars created will balance out with the costs of carrying the partner in years when his contribution is on the decline.

Analysis of the long-term compensation prospects for this hypothetical service partner requires constructing a simple economic model and using it to determine how much the firm can afford to compensate the partner over his entire career, if the years of excess contribution are to completely offset those years in which his compensation and overhead exceed the revenue he produces. In theory, the model is a zero-sum game, in which all gains (that is, years of excess contribution) are exactly offset by losses (that is, years in which the partner is carried). In constructing the model, consideration is given to the fact that billable hours tend to decline slowly with advancing age. The model also reflects the effects of inflation on the firm's hourly rate structure and its administrative costs.

Simply stated, the model measures the cumulative contribution of the partner over his career and seeks to determine a percentage increase in compensation that will fully distribute all excess values (that is, drive cumulative contribution to zero) by retirement age. The model assumes that the partner builds excess values early in his career and gradually takes them out of the firm later in his career. The model is also based upon the somewhat generous assumption that the firm is able to recoup all the inflationary increase in administrative costs by increasing the partner's hourly rate.

The initial assumptions of the model are as follows:

- ◆ Partners are admitted at age thirty-three and retire at age sixty-five.
- ◆ A partner's work pace gradually declines over his thirty-two-year career, from 1,800 billable hours to 1,200 billable hours by age sixty-five.
- ◆ In the firm's hourly rate structure, a new partner's rate is $170 per hour. It rises by a constant percentage each year to top out at $400 per hour at the peak of the partner's career.
- ◆ Overall administrative costs increase at the rate of 3 percent per year.

If the partner receives no increase in compensation above his $150,000 initial compensation, his career excess contribution could be as high as $1.2 million. This, of course, is unrealistic, because one expects compensation to continue to increase, at least in line with inflation. The interesting question is "how large a percentage increase can the firm afford to pay the partner each year so that he is able to take out all his excess contribution to the firm?"

The somewhat startling conclusion of this analysis is that, under the assumptions set forth above, the very best the pure service partner can hope for is an increase of a little more than 1.4 percent per year—about half the assumed rate of inflation! There are probably few thirty-three-year-old partners, currently making $150,000, to whom the prospect of retiring at age sixty-five earning $230,000 per year will seem appealing, especially with inflation at 3 percent per year. The data and assumptions are typical for the legal profession and the result is a hard sell to both parties. The partner is unhappy with compensation that does not keep pace with inflation and the firm is unhappy with the thought of a career-long investment. If the firm grants the partner annual cost-of-living increases, he will end his career earning $375,000 and the firm will have invested $1.9 million in him!

Certainly some of this model can be adjusted to create a more favorable projection, but there is probably no combination of reasonable assumptions (except for a dramatically increased level of total billable hours—54,000 as compared with 47,000, resulting in declining annual billable hours to just 1,575) that would allow for compensation to hold even with the rate of inflation. One alternative—increasing the billing rate more aggressively than assumed—presupposes a change in market conditions and represents, in the opinion of some, a highly limited possibility.

The inevitable conclusions from this analysis are as follows:

- If the only contribution a partner makes to the firm is to work hard for much of his or her career, the best the partner can hope to achieve is declining compensation in real terms.
- To dramatically improve his or her lot, the partner must either work much harder and longer, or find other ways to create incremental value.
- Over the long term, every dollar of excess contribution generated by a partner from his or her own billable hours must be used to fund the partner's compensation.

To the extent that higher operating costs and increased partner compensation can be passed along to clients in the form of higher rates, the firm can afford to pay the partner more, although client resistance to higher rates limits the firm's ability to do so. Cost control or reduction programs may also provide some room for increasing compensation, but these run the risk of cutting costs so low that the partner's ability to function effectively becomes impaired.

Creating additional value can be achieved in a number of ways. Development of standard work product, exemplars, substantive practice systems, and other techniques that increase productivity and create the opportunity for billing more than standard time value are some examples. If there is more work available to the partner than he can comfortably handle, then delegating to and supervising associates can also create additional value. Of course, developing profitable work for high-quality clients is probably the best way to create value.

The inescapable conclusion is that service providers cannot be paid the difference between their revenues and the cost of overhead to support them. Compensation for these partners must be discounted by the opportunity cost of providing them with work.

### The Pure "Finder"

Most firms look to business origination, either individually or as part of a team effort, as the primary way for a partner to create excess value. But is there such a thing as a pure "finder"—one who performs no legal work per se, but functions only as a business originator? How much can a law firm afford to pay for pure origination?

If the answer to this question is to make sense, one must first accept the earlier premise that the best a pure service provider (that is, one who has no origination of his or her own and works only on firm clients or clients of other partners) can hope to achieve, in terms of percentage increases in compensation, is a rate roughly half the rate of inflation. That premise implies that the profit on all partner hours billed and collected must go to pay the partner and build future values to provide for the time when his or her marginal contribution is negative.

For purposes of illustration, assume the following:

- All lawyers, except the rainmaker, bill and collect an average of 1,600 hours per year.
- Service partners bill at an average rate of $200 per hour.
- The rainmaker's hourly rate is $300.
- Administrative support expenses for partners and associates are $100,000 and $75,000 per lawyer, respectively.
- Benefits and payroll taxes are 15 percent of salaries.
- Operating leverage is maintained at 1.5 associates per partner.
- There are three classes of associates, whose billing rates and salaries are as follows:

| Associate Class | Billing Rate | Salary | Profit @ 1,600 Hrs |
|---|---|---|---|
| Senior | $150 | $80,000 | $73,000 |
| Middle | $125 | $67,000 | $48,000 |
| Junior | $100 | $50,000 | $28,000 |

The first and simplest case is one in which a partner has no billable hours, but is able to generate enough work to keep one and one-half associates busy. Assume that the associates are at the senior level.

Scenario 1, as depicted in Table 1.4, shows that unless a rainmaker generates billable work for herself, she can expect a maximum compensation of only $9,500 from her $360,000 book of business. The scenario gets much worse if one assumes that the associates are in the lower-profit categories. (An interesting aside relates to the situation in which a firm is asked to give up a percentage of fees to an of counsel for access to $360,000 worth of business. In this example, the firm cannot afford to give up more than about 2.6 percent of the total book without incurring a loss, if it costs $100,000 to maintain the of counsel. Most law firms give away the store in this area.)

It is unrealistic, of course, to expect that a rainmaker will have no billable time at all. If the rainmaker also generated enough additional work to provide herself 1,000 hours, for example, the firm could afford to pay her up to $309,500 for her book of business. If the rainmaker's hours were 1,500, her compensation could go as high as $459,500 for her book. Eventually the rain-

**TABLE 1.4**
**Pure "Finder"—Scenario 1**

| | Head Count | Hours | Rates | Income and Expense | Percent of Revenue |
|---|---|---|---|---|---|
| Firm income | | | | | |
| Rainmaker | 1 | 0 | 300 | $0 | |
| Service partners | 0 | 1,600 | 200 | 0 | |
| Associates—senior | 1.5 | 1,600 | 150 | 360,000 | |
| Associates—middle | 0 | 1,600 | 125 | 0 | |
| Associates—junior | 0 | 1,600 | 100 | 0 | |
| Revenue | 2.5 | 960* | 150 | 360,000 | 100.00% |
| Firm compensation output | | | | | |
| Associate salary—senior | 1.5 | | 80,000 | 120,000 | 33.33% |
| Associate salary—middle | 0 | | 67,000 | 0 | |
| Associate salary—junior | 0 | | 50,000 | 0 | |
| Benefits (% of salary) | | | 15% | 18,000 | 5.00% |
| Overhead—associates | 1.5 | | 75,000 | 112,500 | 31.25% |
| Service partner compensation | 0 | | 0 | 0 | |
| Overhead—partners | 1 | | 100,000 | 100,000 | 27.78% |
| Total costs | | | | 350,500 | 97.36% |
| Available for rainmaker compensation | | | | $9,500 | 2.64% |
| Operating leverage | | | | 1.5:1 | |

*Average hours per lawyer.

maker's compensation has to top out, however, unless she is able to continue leveraging herself with more and more associates.

In the above example, each additional senior associate the rainmaker keeps busy creates an additional $73,000 in value available for compensation. The most counterproductive scenario occurs when the rainmaker's top senior associate is admitted to partnership. If operating leverage is to be maintained at 1.5:1, then admitting the senior associate to "service partner" status creates a requirement to find work for 2.5 additional associates!

Table 1.5 illustrates how Scenario 2 might work if the rainmaker generated no hours for herself. In this case, assume that the three associates are split evenly among the three classes.

Scenario 2 permits the rainmaker to generate excess value of $48,450 as compared with $9,500 for Scenario 1, but she must generate an additional $520,000 of new business to make it happen.

To some extent, these two scenarios are not comparable because the associate staff mix differs. Comparing "required origination" and "available values" under the two scenarios, assuming that levels of rainmaker hours vary

**TABLE 1.5**
**Pure "Finder"—Scenario 2**

| | Head Count | Hours | Rates | Income and Expense | Percent of Revenue |
|---|---|---|---|---|---|
| Firm income | | | | | |
| Rainmaker | 1 | 0 | 300 | $0 | |
| Service partners | 1 | 1,600 | 200 | 320,000 | |
| Associates—senior | 1 | 1,600 | 150 | 240,000 | |
| Associates—middle | 1 | 1,600 | 125 | 200,000 | |
| Associates—junior | 1 | 1,600 | 100 | 160,000 | |
| Revenue | 5 | 1,280 | 143* | 920,000 | 100.00% |
| Firm compensation output | | | | | |
| Associate salary—senior | 1 | | 80,000 | 80,000 | |
| Associate salary—middle | 1 | | 67,000 | 67,000 | |
| Associate salary—junior | 1 | | 50,000 | 50,000 | 5.43% |
| Benefits (% of salary) | | | 15% | 29,550 | 3.21% |
| Overhead—associates | 3 | | 75,000 | 225,000 | 24.46% |
| Service partner compensation | 1 | | 220,000 | 220,000 | 23.91% |
| Overhead—partners | 2 | | 100,000 | 200,000 | 21.74% |
| Total costs | | | | 871,550 | 94.73% |
| Available for rainmaker compensation | | | | $49,450 | 5.27% |
| Operating leverage | | | | 1.5:1 | |

*Average blended or effective rate per lawyer.

and that all associates are at the middle level, yields other interesting results, as shown in Table 1.6.

If the practice will support only 1.5:1 leverage, the rainmaker must contribute two or three times the business book to support herself and a service partner. And she creates very little excess value in doing so. Is it any wonder why niche practices are difficult to force beyond the threshold stage of one partner and a comfortable number of associates?

**TABLE 1.6**
**Comparison of Scenario 1 and Scenario 2**

| Rainmaker Hours | Scenario 1 | | Scenario 2 | |
|---|---|---|---|---|
| | Required Origination | Available Values | Required Origination | Available Values |
| 0 | $300,000 | ($28,075) | $ 920,000 | $ 43,850 |
| 1,000 | 600,000 | 271,925 | 1,220,000 | 343,850 |
| 1,500 | 750,000 | 421,925 | 1,370,000 | 493,850 |
| 1,800 | 840,000 | 551,925 | 1,460,000 | 583,850 |

Properly stated, the conclusion for this analysis is as follows: The most a law firm can afford to pay a rainmaker—over and above the profits derived from her own billable hours—is the marginal profit derived from the associates the rainmaker can keep busy, regardless of how many partners she occupies.

These examples and scenarios are meant to be provocative. In reality, especially in the short run, rainmakers can produce excess values, particularly when the firm is in an asset-driven posture (that is, has more lawyers than needed to service the work available). One can argue that the rainmaker is getting no credit for sopping up excess capacity in the partner and associate ranks. That argument may play in the short run, but as a long-run strategy, it will not work because it never allows the firm to ask the tough question: "Who are these people and why are they here?"

The analysis is also based on assumptions about associate staffing that, if changed, could produce better results. For example, if the rainmaker used only senior associates, she would fare much better because the profit margin on senior associates is higher. The trade-off for that, of course, is a higher average hourly rate and higher cost to the client.

### Final Observations

These illustrations are meant to be extreme, which is often necessary to make a point. The inescapable conclusions are as follows:

- ◆ Law firms cannot afford too many pure service partners. All partners must contribute excess value in some way, by supervising associates (permitting greater leverage), creating opportunities to bill more than the time value of the work, or contributing to generation of the business base.
- ◆ Rainmakers must produce their own billable values to justify higher compensation.
- ◆ Admitting pure service partners puts an extraordinary burden on firm rainmakers—a fact that they have neither willingly accepted nor generally understood in the past.
- ◆ The most valuable partners are those who offer a balance of skills: worker, delegator, supervisor, and rainmaker.

## Allocating Large Success or Premium Fees

Yes, the traditional bill-by-the-hour method is still the mainstay of the profession. However, law firms and clients continue to explore the possibilities of alternate pricing mechanisms, including flat or fixed fees, retainers, discounted hourly rate and success fees, traditional contingent fees, reverse contingent fees, capped and premium hourly rate fees, and the like. (Readers who would like to explore the topic of pricing mechanisms should obtain *Winning Alternatives to the Billable Hour: Strategies That Work,* edited by James A. Calloway and Mark A. Robertson and *The Essential Formbook: Comprehensive Management Tools for Lawyers* by Gary A. Munneke and Anthony E. Davis; both are published by the ABA.) The intent of such pricing models is:

- ◆ To align fees more closely with the client's perception of value received for the service rendered
- ◆ To take the surprise out of legal fee bills, co-opting legal auditors and others who make a career of ferreting out inconsistencies, apparent overcharges, and similar items in traditional legal invoices
- ◆ To align the law firm's profit incentive more closely with the client's

Today's law firm is likely to have a mixture of pricing models operating simultaneously. Practices such as intellectual property litigation, workout and asset recovery, mass tort litigation, and others are hoping to create extraordinary value for their clients and for themselves. In so doing they are using pricing arrangements that shift risk and reward and raise questions of fair compensation. The answers require analysis of such success-premium fees outside the context of an ongoing practice. In everyday practice, the apportionment of success-premium fees must be developed within the overall context of the firm's existing compensation system, the firm's historical win-loss experience with special pricing, the portability of practices, market forces, and the like. The following case study is drawn from a real-life set of facts, where case acceptance was a firm decision.

## Case Study

This case study raises the use of three theories to assist a firm in working through a success-fee allocation: investment recovery, capital costs, and return for risk assumed.

## Background

Butcher, Baker and Chandler is a fifty-lawyer firm with seventeen equity partners. The firm has a substantial corporate finance and transactional practice, as well as a litigation department that handles big-ticket commercial and securities litigation. About eight years ago, Newton Baker, the firm's principal trial lawyer, successfully defended a groundbreaking, high-visibility, intellectual property infringement suit involving computer software licensing, thereby establishing the firm as a major player in the area. As a result, there has been a steady stream of contacts and case referrals with huge sums of money at stake.

In 1991, the firm agreed to take its first case on contingency—a technology licensing dispute in which the plaintiff sought $20 million in back royalties and prejudgment interest. The fee arrangement was a straight one-third contingent fee that would cover all services and costs advanced. Since that time, the firm has accepted four additional contingent-fee matters on similar terms, all involving substantial claims. When accepted, not one case was deemed an easy win.

In 1995, Baker and his team—one additional partner (Melanie Hamilton), two associates, and two paralegals—won an $18 million jury award in the first case, resulting in a $6 million contingent fee for the firm, which was collected in 1996. Table 1.7 depicts the resources expended by the firm over the life of the case.

Over the course of the case, the firm financed all client costs advanced. Costs advanced in conjunction with the other four cases presently total $625,000 and are likely to amount to more than $1 million before the cases are resolved.

Each year the firm develops a profit plan and, based upon financial projections, computes a standard hourly rate schedule. The firm takes into account direct compensation and benefits, overhead and infrastructure costs, and a target profit margin of 35 percent. The hourly rates computed during the planning process are viewed as guideline rates. Within certain limits, each partner may adjust actual billing upward or downward from the guideline value of time spent on a matter. On average, the firm realizes 95 percent of its guideline rates.

## The Problem

Newt Baker went to the partnership and asked that the $6 million fee be allocated outside the firm's normal profit allocation system and that substantial bonuses be paid to those who served on the trial team. The partnership agreed; however, although the partners reached consensus on the amounts to be paid the associates and paralegals, they failed to agree on a rationale for determining a fair allocation of the fee among the partners. Baker's profit-sharing percentage is 8 percent and Hamilton's is 4 percent.

**TABLE 1.7**
**Resources Expended**

| Year | Time Value | Costs Advanced | Total |
|------|-----------|----------------|-------|
| 1991 | $    55,000 | $    2,000 | $    57,000 |
| 1992 | 765,000 | 90,000 | 855,000 |
| 1993 | 815,000 | 120,000 | 935,000 |
| 1994 | 900,000 | 95,000 | 995,000 |
| 1995 | 250,000 | 10,000 | 260,000 |
| 1996 | 20,000 | 5,000 | 25,000 |
| Total | $2,805,000 | $322,000 | $3,127,000 |

### Resolution

The partnership has recognized that the trial team earned a special bonus because of the result achieved from its extraordinary efforts, unique expertise, and creativity. Because the question of merit is not in dispute, the firm should first address the issue of what constitutes fair compensation for the firm. The partners who worked on the case will receive compensation in two ways: once through the normal distribution of profits and again through a special bonus distribution. Thus, they will share in whatever sums are allocated to the firm.

Few, if any, would dispute the proposition that the firm should be paid for the value of time invested in the case and be reimbursed for the costs advanced. There should be little debate about the proper valuation of costs advanced, but there may be some question about the proper valuation of time expended on the case. There are three distinct possibilities, as follows:

a. Value time charges at 65 percent of standard rates, to reimburse the firm for direct cost and overhead only
b. Value time charges at 95 percent of standard rates, to reflect the firm's normal realization experience
c. Value time charges at 100 percent of standard rates, to provide the firm with a guideline profit on the invested time

The first alternative ignores the opportunity cost of assigning resources to the contingency matter. Presumably, if the firm had not accepted the case, the lawyers who worked on it would have been productively occupied on other matters. The difference between the full rates and the straight-cost rates reflects the normal profit margin that the firm would have earned by assigning the lawyers to other cases. Normal profit in this case becomes the measure of opportunity cost.

The fact that the firm normally recovers 95 percent of guideline rates, on average, may or may not be relevant. The goal should be to afford the firm a normal profit for the commitment of resources. The relevant question is "what profit would the same lawyers have generated if they worked on cases that represent the next best use of their time?" If the firm was accustomed to realizing 110 percent of standard rates on hourly cases in this area, then the appropriate value for the time would be at guideline rates, plus 10 percent. If other similar cases realized only 85 percent, then a 15 percent discount would be appropriate. Lacking additional information, it is best to value the time at full guideline rates.

In considering a proper allocation of values, it is important to recognize that the capital of the firm supported the case for nearly six years. Costs were advanced, salaries were paid, infrastructure was funded, and partners deferred compensation—all to support the matter. Like the lawyers assigned to the case, the money invested in the case has alternative uses. The firm should be compensated for the estimated income the capital could have earned if it had been invested elsewhere. The tricky issue is to determine the rate of return that would fairly compensate the firm for supplying the capital.

One way to compensate for the use of capital is to apply a rate that reflects the firm's cost of borrowing. This method presumes that the firm would have borrowed to finance the case if it lacked the capital to carry it. One might rightly question the wisdom of borrowing money to support a contingent-fee case with a highly uncertain outcome. However, the use of debt might permit the firm to spread the cost of the investment over a greater number of years, thereby making it economically possible to pursue the case. Furthermore, the facts of this matter indicate that the firm financed the case and deferred compensation. Applying a cost-of-borrowing analysis is merely one way to compute a rough estimate of the cost of financing the case.

An alternate method is to estimate the return that could have been earned had equivalent funds been invested in some other similarly risky instrument. This analysis presumes that one can easily measure comparative risk between two alternative investments. It also presumes that one can find alternate investment choices that have the same risk profile as a contingent-fee case. The easy way out of this dilemma is to reimburse the firm for the use of capital at a presumably risk-free rate of return (such as five-year treasury securities) and make an allowance for risk separately from the allowance for capital cost (see below). Assuming that the proper rate of return is determined to be 8.5 percent per annum, the capital cost reimbursement portion associated with the firm's investment in the matter amounts to $1,151,500.

At this point in the analysis, there remains $1,721,500 of the fee to be allocated (the original $6 million, less the investment of $3,127,000 and capital costs of $1,151,500). The firm has been reimbursed for its investment, which allows for a normal profit, and for the carrying cost of the case, based on a risk-free rate.

When it accepted the contingent-fee matter, the firm assumed a risk that all partners shared. If the trial team had lost the case, all partners would have shared in the loss. Fortunately, Baker's team won. Nevertheless, the firm should receive some compensation, over and above the recovery of its investment and capital costs, for taking the risk in the first place.

There are many ways to allocate the remaining fee and to recognize the shared risk. A simple solution would be to share the remaining premium of $1,721,500 equally between the firm and the trial team, or according to some other negotiated proportion. Although some may criticize this approach as being arbitrary and unscientific, negotiated settlements are often preferable because everyone feels equally dissatisfied with the result.

Another solution might be to equalize the profits per partner between the firm and the trial team. For example, implicit in the standard value of time is a 35 percent profit margin, which translates into $981,750 of normal profit. To this add the $1,151,500 in case financing costs. The resulting profit of $2,133,250 represents a profit per partner of $125,485 for the seventeen partners—Baker and Hamilton included. Equalizing the profits means that a special bonus would be allocated to the trial team: the two partners would receive an aggregate bonus of $250,971 and the firm would keep the remainder to pay bonuses to the other members of the trial team and compensate itself for risk. This method appears a little less arbitrary, but it is still fairly unscientific.

A third possibility would be to model the risk-reward allocation on a stock market analogy. The idea is to compare the following: (1) the annual percentage rate of return earned by the firm from taking the case, and (2) an equivalent return that could have been earned by investing the case resources in a moderately risky investment portfolio. The market return is intended to compensate the firm for risk. Any premium over the market return is presumed to have been earned by the trial team.

For example, assume that an investor purchased stocks in the same pattern as the firm invested resources in the case, and collected $6 million when selling the stock at the end of six years. The investor would have earned a return of 18.25 percent per annum, which presumably includes some allowance for the time value of money and an additional allowance for taking the risk in the first place.

Assuming that 8.5 percent represents a risk-free return for the use of capital, then the portion of the overall return that represents compensation for assuming the risk of the case is 9.75 percent (that is, 18.25 percent less 8.5 percent). According to published stock indices, a person who invested in the S&P 500 stocks in 1991 and sold in 1996 would have earned a return of about 15.25 percent. Deducting the 8.5-percent risk-free return leaves a 6.75-percent return to compensate for risk. Indeed, if the firm had been this hypothetical investor, it would have earned 15.25 percent on its money, rather than the 18.25 percent it actually earned on the case. The excess return of three percent can be construed to apply to the extra value added by the trial team. In rough numbers, this would mean allocating 70 percent (roughly 6.75 percent divided by 9.75 percent) of the remaining premium to the firm and 30 percent to the two trial partners. Thus the firm would share $1,048,784, and the two trial partners would receive an extra bonus of $516,450. Here again, the firm would have to determine the amount of bonuses to be paid to the associates and paralegals on the trial team.

The analysis attempts to identify the various elements that should be considered on a case-by-case basis, and then to quantify the results and provide a template for similar calculations. Note that this analysis is focused on a single fee result from a single matter. In practice, one would consider other relevant factors, such as the following:

◆ The firm's historical experience with contingent matters handled by the trial team (simply put, the firm should consider the record of the portfolio before allocating success fees for a single case)
◆ The ongoing portfolio of contingent-fee cases where future losses are possible (a reserve against that potential might be warranted, with ultimate allocation held until the portfolio value is known)
◆ The stature and ultimately the mobility of the trial team (this is a competitive market for talent, and such external influences must always be considered)
◆ Rogue lawyers who leave and take the case with them on the eave of victory (this scenario is not altogether unknown; the firm should prepare for the possibility)

Table 1.8 summarizes the apportionment of the fee, assuming the market risk approach is adopted.

The non-trial-team partners each will take nearly $200,000 in a bonus. Baker and Hamilton will earn more, with that having been balanced against the shared risk and support they received during the heavy-lifting years. And the firm has amassed a $2 million investment pool in recovered costs, ready for future deployment or as a reserve against future losses.

## Rewarding the Stars

How does a firm keep those individuals whose talent, personality, and leadership set the tone for the organization? Some would say, "Overpay them." Many

**TABLE 1.8**
**Apportionment of the Fee, Assuming a Market Risk Approach**

|  | Total | 15 Partners | Baker | Hamilton |
|---|---|---|---|---|
| Costs advanced | $ 322,000 | $ 283,360 | $ 25,760 | $ 12,880 |
| Time value at cost | 1,823,250 | 1,604,460 | 145,860 | 72,930 |
| Cost recovered | 2,145,250 | 1,887,820 | 171,620 | 85,810 |
| Normal profit | 981,750 | 863,940 | 78,540 | 39,270 |
| Capital cost | 1,151,500 | 1,013,320 | 92,120 | 46,060 |
| Risk premium | 1,191,800 | 1,048,784 | 95,344 | 47,672 |
| Skill premium | 529,700 | 0 | 353,133 | 176,567 |
| Case profit | 3,854,750 | 2,926,044 | 619,137 | 309,569 |
| Total (cost recovered plus case profit) | $6,000,000 | $4,813,864 | $790,757 | $395,379 |
| Apportionment of case profit | 100.0% | 76% | 16% | 8% |
| Case profit per partner | 226,750 | 195,070 | 619,137 | 309,569 |

believe that a firm is better off when it pays higher than the market, no matter who the employee. Experience shows that talent is just too difficult to find and keep to allow it to be swept away by a better offer. Moreover, the additional energy and loyalty a firm buys when it "wows" someone with compensation is far more than the dollars used.

But many of the most important and talented people in an organization do what they do *not* because of the compensation system or for more money, but because their internal gyroscopes dictate that such behavior is critical for success and they are success driven (as opposed to money driven). Do not take that statement as an opportunity to pay less. But do realize that these individuals are not likely to alter their behavior because of pay systems. They expect a pay system to recognize the value of their efforts and to pay them accordingly.

Generally, money will not draw them away (though money may be necessary to get them away). Key people may turn down many offers of more money for many reasons. One is that they consider themselves to be owners of their law firms and not just employees who also happen to be owners—a subtle turn of words representing a powerful difference in thinking. How many times have senior partners "left money on the table?" They do it to help maintain harmony among the troops and to set a tone of inclusion.

Remuneration for these individuals comes in the form of the freedom they enjoy. They are excited by the challenges presented by their clients and the market. Competitors who provide them with bigger challenges, substantially better resources, or opportunities to learn or develop new skills are the ones who have a chance to get their attention.

## Other Owner Compensation Issues

### Distributions

In a partnership, partners may be assigned draws that represent a prospective share of profits (as defined in a partnership tax return). This means that if there is a shortfall, some of the draws will have to be repaid to the firm to maintain the firm's capital. Shareholders of professional corporations are assigned salaries. The term implies that the full amount is earned and none of it is returnable. A salary, however, may be withheld by the firm if cash flow is insufficient to cover all overhead and shareholder compensation (provided their agreements so stipulate). Many law firms, partnerships, and professional corporations alike got into trouble during economic recession by borrowing to sustain owner compensation when cash flows began to falter. See the related short piece in Appendix 2, which discusses the impact of law firm borrowing on compensation.

The amounts to be paid to owners should be agreed upon, and the time of issue regulated. In some law firms, partners are permitted to obtain payments at their own volition, which can cause disorder in a firm's finances. Some partners may draw out (and do draw out) more than they are entitled to receive, leaving nothing for the others. Moreover, such an arrangement tends to create havoc with cash flow planning.

Further, salaries and draws should be conservatively set. This helps provide cash reserves to cover cash flow imbalances throughout the year or unexpected dips in profits. It is easier on the firm and the workers if paychecks are not missed and capital calls avoided. Concurrent with this theme, conservative salaries and draws force some measure of discipline on the owners' lifestyles, and can help prevent overextension if the firm's numbers falter. Finally, if the firm desires a successful incentive-based income distribution plan, it must make the incentive payments significant in relation to overall compensation. Conservative base compensation is a means to achieve that end.

Special distributions or bonuses may be paid any time management determines that the firm has an adequate reserve of cash to meet its needs and provide for some contingencies. Generally, law firms pay distributions (beyond draws or bonuses) to owners quarterly or annually. The deciding factor appears to be the form of organization. Partners need to make quarterly estimated income tax payments and they tend to distribute profits in accordance with those cycles. Shareholders usually do not need to make quarterly payments, as they have income tax withheld from each paycheck. Professional corporations, therefore, tend to pay bonuses on an annual basis.

On average, 60 percent of total compensation is paid out as a draw or salary, and another 4.5 percent provides benefits. The remaining 35.5 percent is paid out as bonus or distribution. In partnerships, 8 percent of total compensation is distributed in quarterly tax draws, reducing profit distribution to 27.5 percent.[12]

## Tax Treatment of Partners and Shareholders

Partners are self-employed individuals. The partnership is not a separate taxable entity, but rather a pass-through entity through which items of income, loss, deduction, and credit pass to the partners. Members of limited liability companies (LLCs) are generally treated like partners for tax purposes, with some special considerations that are beyond the scope of this text.

Shareholders are employees. The professional corporation is a separate taxable entity. It can pay tax, and will, if income is left in the corporation at year-end. An exception is a professional corporation that has elected to be taxed as a partnership ("S" election). In that instance, shareholders with more than 2 percent are treated as partners in connection with the application of fringe benefits.

There are differences in the way such compensation is treated for tax purposes and the way it is most likely reported by an owner. Comparisons between shareholder and partner compensation must be made with care to ensure that an apples-to-apples analysis is performed.

In partnership accounting, partner profits include payments made for health, disability, and life insurance, as well as pension plans. For example, a partner with a $200,000 share of profit may experience a cash flow of the following:

| | |
|---|---|
| Paid out to insurance benefits | $ 6,000 |
| Contributed to pension plan | $ 30,000 |
| Paid out in cash or retained as capital | $164,000 |
| Reportable earnings | $200,000 |

The partner could deduct the amount paid into the pension plan, a percentage of the self-employed health insurance premiums, and one-half of the self-employment tax owed on his or her individual income tax return.

If this same individual were a shareholder in a professional corporation, his or her reported income would be $157,471. At first glance, it would appear that the shareholder was paid less. This is not the case. An earnings summary explains why:

**Earnings Summary**
**(Year ending December 31, 2xxx)**

| | |
|---|---|
| Salary and bonuses paid (reportable earnings) | $157,471 |
| Group life, health, and disability insurance premiums (paid by firm, not reportable as income) | $ 6,000 |
| Medical reimbursement plan payments (paid by firm, not reportable as income) | $ 1,000 |
| Pension plan contribution (paid by firm, not reportable as income) | $ 30,000 |
| FICA taxes paid by employer | $ 5,529 |
| | $200,000 |

It is important for all employees to receive such statements, so they understand that there is considerable investment beyond salary and bonus.

# Summary

Law firms continually examine their pay practices. Unfortunately, many still approach their assessments by mimicking the practices of others. Although this may level the playing field in terms of compensation practice, it does little to create or support substantial competitive advantage. There is a growing movement toward objective merit-based systems that are integrated with individual partner goal setting and peer review programs. Pure lockstep and formula systems are giving ground to more consciously managed systems, which are based upon a combination of both subjective and objective observations and which recognize compensation as an important motivational factor in professional practice.

The migration toward managed systems for partner compensation has occurred gradually over the 1980s and 1990s. Lockstep and formula systems alike, while retaining some of their basic structures, have been modified to allow for more conscious slotting of partners. Movement up the lockstep ladder each year is no longer guaranteed and some partners are being frozen in place or moved down. Formula-driven systems have become less rigid with the introduction of subjective bonus pools and other devices that allow firm managers to adjust for the aberrations that formulas inevitably create.

Now firms are beginning to realize that managed compensation practices have limitations. For example, some individuals may not respond (or not respond well) to compensation as a behavior management tool.[13] The realization that the biggest contributors function *not* because of compensation, but rather because of an inherent sense of what it takes to be successful, has forced decision makers to respond by recognizing such contributions. Those who are underperforming may not respond to compensation-based behavior management. Poor performance typically results in reduced compensation, which in turn produces even lower performance. A downward spiral is created from which a reasonable solution is not likely.

The new merit-based systems require that managers develop a clear statement of the subjective and objective measures of partner performance, ensure that the criteria are consistent with the firm's strategic objectives, and forge a broad consensus among the rank-and-file partners in support of the criteria. Managers must also have a clear understanding of how different partners contribute in different ways to the economic success of the firm. Though business development skills are important, many firms may be overcompensating rainmakers. Others may be overcompensating partners who originate no business, but instead service the clients of others. Understanding the economics of the two types of activities is essential to developing a balanced system of partner compensation. Above all, firms must strive to build cadres of partners with balanced skills: lawyering, managing, and rainmaking. All three are vitally important to the long-term success of the firm.

## Endnotes

1. *Compensation Systems in Private Law Firms Survey* (Newtown Square, PA: Altman Weil Publications, Inc., 2003).

2. Managing partners invested 55 percent of their time attending to the business affairs of their law firms in 1994, up from 47 percent in 1992. However, by 1997, management activities had slipped below 40 percent. This is more reflective of the pressing work of clients than a decline in needed management for the firm. *Managing Partner and Executive Director Survey* (Newtown Square, PA: Altman Weil Publications, Inc., 1992, 1994, 1997, 2002).

3. *Compensation Systems in Private Law Firms Survey* (Newtown Square, PA: Altman Weil Publications, Inc., 2003).

4. Varies by size of firm and the year in which it was measured. The top two are clearly differentiated from the remaining objective criteria.

5. *Compensation Systems in Private Law Firms Survey* (Newtown Square, PA: Altman Weil Publications, Inc., 2003).

6. Ibid.

7. "Law Office Organization," *American Bar Association Journal,* May, June, July, August 1940.

8. *Compensation Systems in Private Law Firms Survey* (Newtown Square, PA: Altman Weil Publications, Inc., 2003).

9. Ibid.

10. *Survey of Law Firm Economics* (Newtown Square, PA: Altman Weil Publications, Inc., various years).

11. "Law Office Organization," *American Bar Association Journal,* May, June, July, August 1940.

12. *Compensation Systems in Private Law Firms Survey* (Newtown Square, PA: Altman Weil Publications, Inc., 2003).

13. Jim Collins in *Good to Great* and David Maister in *Practice What You Preach* concluded that compensation systems did not drive behavior. Rather decisions about which people to compensate in the first place (Collins) and the quality of the decisions themselves (Maister) were the important considerations in driving behavior and performance.

# *Of Counsel Compensation*

## 2

## Overview

Look at a sample of law firm letterhead or listings in *Martindale-Hubbell* and you will usually find lawyers listed as "of counsel." In the late 1960s, the significance of the listing was usually quite clear. It meant "Here is a former partner who is either retired or is scaling down toward full retirement." Now one sees a variety of titles in use, such as "senior attorney," "special counsel," "senior counsel," or the elegantly simple "counsel." Each title presumably signifies some kind of relationship other than the traditional partner or associate, but the lack of standardization of terminology leaves one at a loss to divine precisely what a law firm means by making the distinction. In many cases, the lack of clarity has been intentional. However, there were an estimated seventeen thousand lawyers practicing in an of counsel capacity in 2000, and the number is likely to grow rapidly over the next twenty years. Law firms should carefully consider adopting protocols for such lawyers, as they are likely to become a more significant presence in a maturing legal market.

In practice, of counsel has been used to mean one of two states of practice:

1. One that is in transition
2. One that is segregated from the mainstream practice of the law firm
   - The most common uses have been to signify one of the following:

◆ A partner or former partner has retired or is scaling down to retired status. This is probably the purest use of the title to describe transition.

◆ A lateral partner candidate and the law firm operate under a "living-together" arrangement while each scrutinizes the other and ponders the prospect of eventual full partnership status. This usage incorporates concepts of both transition and segregation, as there is an expectation that the lawyer's status will eventually evolve into full partnership.

◆ A lawyer's practice has been isolated from the firm for ethical or business reasons. For example, certain states require that lobbying activities be isolated from other practice areas so that partners who do the lobbying work do not share fees with others who may have an economic interest in the outcome of legislative developments. In other cases, the lawyer or the firm may want to maintain permanent of counsel status to create separate profit centers for division of profits or other business purposes. Similarly, a lawyer may wish to retain independent contractor status to retain certain advantages under tax laws. This usage is purely one connoting segregation.

On May 10, 1990, the ABA Standing Committee on Ethics and Professional Responsibility adopted and issued Formal Opinion 90-357, which governs when and how law firms use the title "of counsel." In doing so, the committee included the most common variations on the themes listed above for of counsel status.

The ABA has recognized the importance of bringing clarity to this issue, and has an excellent resource guide published by the Senior Lawyers Division, entitled *The Of Counsel Agreement.* The second edition of this book was published in 1998. The book contains Formal Opinion 90-357, discusses issues relevant after the Opinion, provides guidance on a myriad of issues regarding using of counsel relationships in a law firm, and provides sample agreements. A disk containing the agreements in electronic form is included.

Successfully creating an of counsel relationship requires that both parties do their homework and be very thorough and careful in how they agree on the terms of the relationship. For starters, all such relationships should be governed by a written contract between the parties. At a minimum, the agreement should cover the following:

◆ The purpose of the relationship and the parties' expectations concerning benefits to be gained

◆ Specific duties and responsibilities of both parties

- The term of the agreement and conditions under which it is subject to extension or renewal
- Guidelines for client acceptance, work allocation, client billing protocols, and control of files
- Agreements regarding ownership of files and intellectual property
- The method of compensation, including timing of payments
- Conflict-checking policies and procedures
- Provisions by which either party may terminate the agreement
- Consequences of termination of the agreement, as they relate to unfinished work-in-progress, uncollected fees, retention of files, reuse of intellectual property, and continuing contact with joint clients
- Indemnification terms and conditions, confidentiality provisions, and any other rights of either party that are retained or limited

# Of Counsel Compensation

Of counsel compensation must be considered in the context of the jurisdiction's ethics rules. Once these issues are identified and addressed, then the nature of the relationship between the of counsel and the firm can be considered. Elements of that relationship include overhead allocation, fee attribution, work sharing, funding of joint promotional expenses, and the like. Many firms provide for a very simple structure, while others engage in more complex arrangements. The best approach is very much dependent upon the nature of the of counsel arrangement.

## Scaling Down

If the arrangement is one where an existing partner is scaling down to retired status, then there is an opportunity to append the of counsel compensation structure to the firm's existing partner compensation program. There are three philosophies with such a program—look back, look forward, and a combination of the two.

A look-back philosophy is characterized by a desire to provide certainty to the retiring partner that compensation either will not be adversely affected during transition or is affected in a planned and deliberate way. Such an approach is generally suggested when a partner is asked to transfer relationships to younger partners, particularly when a book of business is a prime factor in compensation decisions. This is a good approach in that there is certainty for the individual. However, the firm has no assurance of the results of the efforts or that the plan will be implemented as originally structured. Many a law firm has chafed at the five-year program of payments that ended up coupled to an eighteen-month phase-out of interest and contribution from the individual.

A very simple look-back approach is to define the reduced-workload expectations that come with corresponding reductions in compensation. The following depicts an institutionalized program[1] used to wind down a partner to retired status.

The of counsel position is a period of transition for the individual and the firm. Of counsel status is usually a five-year period of steadily declining direct total contribution to the benefit of the law firm in terms of hours, with a changing focus away from billable work and new business development toward external and internal relations. Each of counsel may propose a scheduled wind-down that meets the individual's personal needs and those of the firm. The firm will approve such proposals provided that it is in the interest of the firm and not detrimental to the firm's mission of serving its clients. The general thinking of the firm in this regard is:

| | |
|---|---|
| Year one (age 65) | 90% of 2,000 hours = 1,800 hours |
| Year two (age 66) | 75% of 2,000 hours = 1,750 hours |
| Year three (age 67) | 60% of 2,000 hours = 1,200 hours |
| Year four (age 68) | 40% of 2,000 hours = 800 hours |
| Year five (age 69) | 20% of 2,000 hours = 400 hours |
| Year six (age 70) | Fully retired |

Compensation will be adjusted downward in proportion to the reduced commitment (for example: at age 67, with 60% commitment, compensation is 60% of pre-wind-down levels).

If the firm uses a point or percentage system, then the number of points or the percentage is reduced. If the firm wants to lock in the payments, it could set forth a salary schedule for each year. It is important to provide the opportunity for additional compensation for business origination or other contributions that materially exceed the agreed-upon expectations.

A look-forward philosphy is one where the method of calculating future compensation is established, but the amount is not known because it is determined by the results of the individual's efforts. The living-together arrangement described below is an example of how one might look forward. A typical program is the 40/20/40 allocation where 40 percent of each fee goes to overhead, 20 percent of each fee goes to the source of the work, and 40 percent of the fee goes to the actual performers of the work. Critics point out that there are weaknesses in any pure percentage approach at the extremes. If production and origination are too low, then the allocated amounts do not cover a reasonable share of overhead. Conversely, if production and origination are too high, the allocated amounts turn the overhead assessment into a firm profit center. While true, few individuals need worry about the latter when scaling back is the objective. For the firm, the "cost" of absorbing the under-allocated overhead is most likely an affordable accommodation provided that reasonable overhead commitments are made.

Some firms have adopted a combination approach providing some minimum threshold of look-back certainty and offering a look-forward opportunity for the individual to earn more. This works well as a transition element for a firm that has a look back program and seeks to replace it with a look forward program.

### Living-Together Arrangements

This of counsel relationship incorporates concepts of both transition and segregation. It is important that the compensation arrangement yield a result that allows the individual to be inserted into the firm's partner compensation structure at the end of the "break-in" or "getting-to-know-you" period.

Most typical is an agreement that provides for an assumption of overhead and a percentage of fees produced. Fee allocations vary, based on the source of the business and who performs the service, and generally provide the following percentages of collected fees to the of counsel:

- ◆ Of counsel originates and services the work: 40%–66%
- ◆ Of counsel originates, and the firm services the work: 10%–33%
- ◆ The firm originates, and of counsel services the work: 33%–50%

It is preferable to use collected fees as the basis for compensating of counsel. However, issues of adjustments (premium or discount), allocation of payments to fees and costs, and billing protocols must be determined and set forth in the agreement. A transition cutoff should also be provided, which stipulates how matters billed but not yet collected will be handled when the of counsel is brought into the firm as a partner.

### Isolated Practice

This type of arrangement represents a pure segregation of practices, for either ethical or business reasons. It is therefore imperative that the economic arrangement complies with the segregation intent of the arrangement.

Overhead should be divided into basic direct and indirect costs. The parties should absorb direct costs on a transaction basis. They should share indirect costs on some reasonable basis (square footage, per lawyer, per fee earner, per partner, or per capita) or through some weighted allocation method. Fees can be allocated using a breakdown as shown above in the living-together example.

### Endnote

1. Portion of a program developed for a client.

# Associate Compensation

## 3

## Overview

For purposes of this text, the term "associate" means a lawyer employed by a law firm in a full-time capacity, without any attributes of ownership. It includes the traditional associate—a lawyer in his or her first five to ten years of practice and on a career track to an ownership interest—as well as the associate who is not on a career track to partnership.

Law schools, no matter how prestigious, produce well-schooled graduates, *not* skilled lawyers. The art and craft of lawyering is learned during several years of training, and by observing and doing. Law firm training historically was a profit center for law firms. Then, starting salaries were quite low (as were the billing rates) and clients paid for the training as the junior lawyer worked on matters. During the 1980s economic conditions changed dramatically. Starting salaries increased significantly. Then came the economic recession of 1990–91 and several years of starting salary stagnation. National average starting salaries in law firms peaked at $50,000 in 1989 and remained there until 1998[1] when they began to rise, and rise rapidly during the peak years of the economic boom. Starting compensation packages of $145,000 made headlines around the nation. Large law firms competed fiercely for talent and the starting salaries in that segment of the market were vastly higher than the national averages.

The shifting associate market is also affected by social and demographic changes in the profession. The profession is aging.

It is also becoming more gender neutral, as the ranks of women in the profession grew rapidly during the 1980s and 1990s. In 1995, females represented only 24 percent of the profession overall, but they were 39 percent of the profession under the age of thirty.[2] Add to the mix generational changes in life and career priorities, and the result is a need to adapt to a labor pool with different expectations and desires.

The typical first full year for an associate usually is an investment for the law firm. By the end of the fourth year, that investment is recovered. However, a law firm generally does not make the one-third profit expected in years gone by. The old formula provided that one-third of an associate's fees should be for his or her compensation, one-third for overhead, and one-third for the firm as profit (that is, fees should be three times compensation). Table 3.1 clearly shows the error in this calculation. The table is produced from 2002 national

**TABLE 3.1**
**Associate Profitability—First Eight Years**

| | Years of Experience | | | | | | | | |
| | Year 1 | Year 2 | Year 3 | Year 4 | Year 5 | Year 6 | Year 7 | Year 8 | Associates as a Group |
|---|---|---|---|---|---|---|---|---|---|
| **Fee Production** | | | | | | | | | |
| Average annual billable hours | 1,557 | 1,808 | 1,847 | 1,869 | 1,834 | 1,880 | 1,894 | 1,860 | 1,842 |
| Average standard billing rate | $145 | $153 | $163 | $172 | $180 | $191 | $193 | $203 | $177 |
| Fee production | $225,765 | $276,624 | $301,061 | $321,468 | $330,120 | $359,080 | $365,542 | $377,580 | $326,034 |
| Average Time Written Off | ($12,643) | ($15,491) | ($16,859) | ($18,002) | ($18,487) | ($20,108) | ($20,470) | ($21,144) | ($18,258) |
| Billable Fees Produced | $213,122 | $261,133 | $284,202 | $303,466 | $311,633 | $338,972 | $345,072 | $356,436 | $307,776 |
| **Cash Receipts** | | | | | | | | | |
| Holdover (1) | $0 | $71,276 | $87,333 | $95,048 | $101,491 | $104,222 | $113,365 | $115,405 | $0 |
| Carry forward (1) | ($71,276) | ($87,333) | ($95,048) | ($101,491) | ($104,222) | ($113,365) | ($115,405) | ($119,206) | $0 |
| Average AR written off | ($7,459) | ($9,140) | ($9,947) | ($10,621) | ($10,907) | ($11,864) | ($12,078) | ($12,475) | ($10,772) |
| Cash receipts | $134,387 | $235,937 | $266,540 | $286,402 | $297,995 | $317,965 | $330,954 | $340,160 | $297,004 |
| **Position Costs** | | | | | | | | | |
| Average overhead (2) | $121,964 | $121,964 | $121,964 | $121,964 | $121,964 | $121,964 | $121,964 | $121,964 | $121,964 |
| Average total compensation (3) | $80,744 | $99,095 | $103,877 | $110,349 | $114,553 | $122,097 | $124,247 | $133,809 | $116,585 |
| Position cost | $202,708 | $221,059 | $225,841 | $232,313 | $236,517 | $244,061 | $246,211 | $255,773 | $238,549 |
| Cash Basis Profit (Loss) | ($68,321) | $14,878 | $40,699 | $54,089 | $61,478 | $73,904 | $84,743 | $84,387 | $58,455 |
| Cash Basis Cum. Profit (Loss) | ($68,321) | ($53,444) | ($12,745) | $41,343 | $102,821 | $176,725 | $261,468 | $345,854 | |
| Cash Basis Margin | -30.3% | 5.4% | 13.5% | 16.8% | 18.6% | 20.6% | 23.2% | 22.3% | 17.9% |
| Accrual Basis Profit (Loss) | $2,955 | $30,934 | $48,414 | $60,531 | $64,209 | $83,047 | $86,783 | $88,187 | $58,455 |
| Accrual Basis Cum. Profit (Loss) | $2,955 | $33,889 | $82,303 | $142,834 | $207,043 | $290,090 | $376,873 | $465,060 | |
| Accrual Basis Margin | 1.3% | 11.2% | 16.1% | 18.8% | 19.5% | 23.1% | 23.7% | 23.4% | 17.9% |
| **Pipeline Calculation** | | | | | | | | | |
| Average unbilled time | $58,024 | 2.1 | Months | | | | | | |
| Average accounts receivable | $52,175 | 1.9 | Months | | | | | | |
| Total pipeline | $110,199 | 4.0 | Months | | | | | | |
| Average gross receipts (AGR) | $329,504 | | | | | | | | |
| Total pipeline/AGR | 33.4% | | | | | | | | |

NOTES:

1. Holdover and carry forward reflect the delay in cash receipts attributed to time keeping, billing and collection policies. This is reflected in the cash receipts "Holdover" and "Carry forward" rows.
2. Average overhead includes all firm expenses, except lawyer and paralegal compensation.
3. Total compensation includes cash, benefits, retirement contributions, and employer taxes.

Source: SURVEY OF LAW FIRM ECONOMICS (Newtown Square, PA: Altman Weil Publications, Inc, 2003).

average survey data[3] and is only an indication of overall economics; it is not what specific firms should strive to achieve. An associate produces a 24 percent margin at his or her peak, and over the associate's career, a law firm should expect an average 18 percent return.

Beyond the starting salary, associate signing bonuses are provided by just under half of the law firms. Eligibility for such bonuses varies greatly, depending on the experience level of the new associate. Signing bonuses had a median value of $5,000 in 2002.

Once an associate is on board, the firm must have a system to evaluate the performance of the individual. Although the first few years of practice may involve more of a lockstep advancement system, after that time individual performance differences begin to surface and must be recognized. Performance evaluations are often granted third-class importance, relegated to the "necessary but evil" paperwork of the firm. This is the wrong approach. Evaluation is critical as a component of the training program, the compensation program, and the admission-to-ownership program. A few firms have found that improper evaluation techniques have come back to haunt them when disgruntled employees take their employers (or former employers) to court. Technology can greatly assist in simplifying, leveling, and enhancing the evaluation process.

After the early years, law firms tend to evaluate their associates using the same criteria that are used for the partners. There are several reasons for this. First, the partners are familiar with the definitions and have reached agreement about their importance and meaning within the firm. Second, the associates are hopefully on a track toward eventual ownership and therefore should be evaluated against that goal. There is no better assessment tool than the criteria the partners apply to themselves. Third, it is relatively simple to apply the standards, as the requisite information is already available.

In practice, the relative importance of criteria changes as an associate gains experience. In the early years, partners look for work ethic, ease of training, and willingness to learn, as well as other factors that determine the associate's ability to "fit" in the firm. As experience is garnered, the partners look more at application of legal knowledge, effectiveness of client counseling, knowledge of clients' industries and businesses, client rapport, efforts to develop business, and community contacts and interests. In the years just before formal consideration for partnership, attributes such as client development, business acumen, willingness and ability to assist new personnel, and leadership skills take on added importance.

Throughout their tenure, associates are evaluated on how well they handle criticism, difficult situations, and demanding clients. Of course, the evaluation also must consider the level of fee receipts produced and how efficiently they are generated.

## Salary Administration

Salary levels vary around the nation. Factors such as firm size, population density, geographic region, and practice specialty all affect salary. For example, smaller firms tend to pay less than larger ones, firms in less-populated areas tend to pay less than those in large cities, and firms in the west north central region† of the United States tend to pay less than those in other areas. Table 3.2 provides an example of the variability of compensation and the different factors considered.

**TABLE 3.2**
**Selected Associate Compensation Data**

|  | *Lower Quartile**  | *Ninth Decile**  |
| --- | --- | --- |
| West North Central region† | $ 74,605 | $121,915 |
| Middle Atlantic region | $127,795 | $181,990 |
| Under 9 lawyers | $ 58,096 | $138,506 |
| Over 150 lawyers | $109,630 | $210,900 |
| Under 250,000 population | $ 76,006 | $143,810 |
| Over 1,000,000 population | $ 98,550 | $179,726 |
| Insured Defense | $ 75,071 | $116,242 |
| Intellectual Property | $140,820 | $250,328 |
| One year of experience | $ 66,821 | $111,412 |
| 8 to 12 years of experience | $102,114 | $189,203 |

*Amounts include W-2 wages plus employer-paid benefits and payroll taxes.
Source: SURVEY OF LAW FIRM ECONOMICS (Newtown Square, PA: Altman Weil Publications, Inc., 2003).

As in most employment, experience is a significant factor in compensation advancement. Experience for lawyers is measured from the first year they are admitted to practice law in any jurisdiction. The rapid increase in starting salaries has actually skewed what would normally be a continuously positive sloping curve (see Illustration 3.1).

However, associate compensation is not an endless series of increases. At some point compensation reaches an upward limit that is difficult to overcome. This is primarily due to the fact that associates should not be profit takers (although some firms allow them to be). As such, they face real economic limits if they sell primarily time (there are only 8,760 total hours in one year, some of which even the most aggressive biller must reserve for other activities), especially with rates already under careful client scrutiny.

---

†North Dakota, South Dakota, Minnesota, Nebraska, Iowa, Kansas and Missouri

**ILL. 3.1**
**Total Compensation—Associates**
**(By years since admission to the Bar, all firms 2002)**

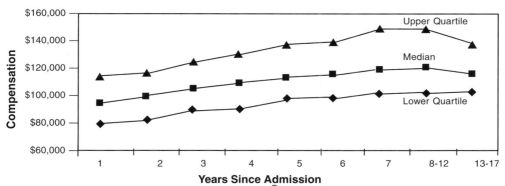

**Years Since Admission**
Source: 2003 *Survery of Law Firm Economics*, Altman Weil® Publications, Inc., Newtown Square, PA 19073.

Salary is the most important component in an associate's compensation package. Bonuses are common. Across the profession, the likelihood of receiving a bonus increases each year, starting at 44 percent and increasing steadily to 76 percent at about the ninth year; then the likelihood decreases over time back to 53 percent. However, there is a wide range of bonus awards. The lowest lower quartile bonus amount was $1,000, while the highest ninth decile bonus amount was $44,258 in 2002. In addition to cash, a benefit package is a significant component of an associate's compensation. A benefit package typically includes health, disability, and life insurance; employer pension contributions; and employer payroll taxes. An average associate's benefit package ranges from $11,472 for first-year admitted associates to $17,620 for very senior, experienced associates. The large difference shows how compensation-based benefits (life insurance, disability insurance, pension contributions, and payroll taxes) affect your total position cost. Health insurance, on the other hand, is simply expensive.

There are three primary approaches to salary administration. The first focuses on years of experience, the second on a career track, and the third on individual contribution (performance). The early years for some firms are purely lockstep, because those firms cannot distinguish among the junior lawyers while they are learning the basic skills of serving client needs.

### *Years-of-Experience Salary Administration*

This approach essentially creates a class-oriented compensation structure. Each year the individual advances along the compensation schedule, and how far he or she progresses from year to year varies according to the differential for the year and any movement of the entire schedule. Performance may or may not come into play other than a decision on retention.

When establishing the initial pay scale, the firm must first determine its market and where it wants to position itself in the market. This book's introduction discusses the concept of a labor market. Each law firm must assess the market in which it competes for associate talent. For most firms it is a regional market. Once the market is determined, survey data should be obtained that can provide information regarding prevailing wage levels in that market or as close a proxy to that market as possible. Based on the market data, the firm should position itself to compete. For example, many employers like to be in the interquartile range (the middle 50 percent). This leaves the bottom 25 percent of prospects as not meeting the standards of the firm and the top 25 percent for someone else. Other firms apply the "80/20 rule" and seek to include 80 percent of the market. Here, they will structure themselves between the first and ninth deciles, leaving to others the 10 percent of the market at either end. Still other firms seek to employ fewer—yet higher caliber—associates. They may position themselves in the market between the median and the ninth decile.

After the firm positions itself in the market, it must examine the client base and other matters to determine the economic realities of its practice. Let's examine a typical midmarket situation. If the firm expects to generate $243,000 in fees from a position (1,800 hours at $150 per hour, with 90 percent realization), and the fee-earner overhead (say $125,000), pension (none initially), benefits (say $8,000), and taxes (say $5,000) equal $138,000, then the salary offer cannot exceed $105,000—just to break even. Most likely, the firm would pay $81,000 in salary for such a position, leaving room for a bonus (say 9 percent or $7,000) and a profit of $17,000 (a 7 percent margin). So much for the "rule of threes," which would say $81,000 in compensation, $81,000 in overhead, and $81,000 in profit on fees of $243,000!

Combining the two analyses described above provides the firm with an indication of the market in which it can compete, and the economically justifiable offer it can make.

Periodically the firm must redetermine appropriate salary ranges, based on the market and the firm's own economic factors. Adjustments to the schedule may not always be possible. In that case, the market may move ahead of the firm. The past several years have forced greater changes at the lower ends of the associate compensation scale, compressing wages because increases could not be made elsewhere. Although perhaps undesirable, adjustments can be driven only by market forces and a firm's ability to adjust its operations to enhance profitability.

A sample small firm salary schedule is shown in Table 3.3. It provides for a minimum and maximum salary for each year. In the first two years, this firm

**TABLE 3.3**
**Sample Associate Salary Schedule for a Small Firm**

| Year | Minimum | Maximum |
|------|---------|---------|
| 1 | $50,000 | $50,000 |
| 2 | $55,000 | $55,000 |
| 3 | $60,000 | $63,000 |
| 4 | $65,000 | $71,000 |
| 5 | $70,000 | $79,000 |
| 6 | $75,000 | $87,000 |
| 7 | $80,000 | $95,000 |

has decided to operate with a lockstep system and not differentiate among its associates. Notice that the ranges eventually overlap; that is, by the fourth year, the maximum for one year is higher than the minimum for the next year. This firm provides for an annual $5,000 increase in the minimum salary. The maximum advances with the minimum for the first three years, and then advances at an annual rate of $8,000. By creating salary ranges, this firm has decided to consider performance as a variable in setting compensation at least within each class.

A firm may choose to ask an individual to leave if performance does not warrant the minimum for his or her class. That would have been the rule ten years ago. Now, more and more firms hold the associate back and see how performance develops. As long as the basic economics of the individual remain profitable and there is sufficient work for the firm to succeed, such a course is acceptable.

## Career-Track Salary Administration

This method is very similar in operation to the years-of-experience salary administration method. The major difference is that individual years of experience are not the focal point. Rather, the firm defines a career track through which the associate may pass. The program recognizes that annual experience differences among associates are less meaningful than skill sets, that law firms must define career tracks for their professional employees, and that "up or out" is not an economically rational strategy in a competitive talent market. This method requires a commitment to individual consideration of performance in setting compensation.

Career-track programs set forth position requirements that include quality and quantity of work, client relations, internal relations, personal qualities, and the like. While experience or tenure are not requirements, the following example provides guidance as to how long one might need to develop at each level. An example of a basic program follows.

## Example Program

*ENTRY-LEVEL ASSOCIATE*

### Qualifications

**Quality of work.** Each entry-level associate is expected to perform accurate, thorough, and timely work; understand the basics of various areas of law; draft routine documents; and negotiate routine matters with little supervision.

**Quantity of work:** Each entry-level associate is expected to work a minimum 2,100 hours per year on behalf of the firm, 1,800 of which are billable and 300 of which are directed toward other firm-approved activities. The senior lawyers and shareholders are responsible for providing sufficient files for an associate to meet this requirement.

**Client relations:** Each entry-level associate should be informed, reliably accurate, and diplomatic in client meetings.

**Personal qualities:** Each entry-level associate should strive to gain the confidence of all other members of the firm, and have a strong work ethic and an ability to balance the requirements of work and personal life.

**Tenure:** A lawyer employed by the firm who has not yet passed the bar exam becomes an entry-level associate upon licensure. An individual typically remains an entry-level associate for the first three years of his or her career.

### Compensation Potential

Entry-level associate salaries currently range from $__,000 to $__,000, per annum. Salary progression is based on improved personal performance. Adjustments to salary are made annually, effective on the employee's anniversary date of employment with the firm.

In addition to salary, an entry-level associate may qualify for a bonus of up to __ percent of annual salary. Bonuses are discretionary, based on both individual and firm performance, and are awarded during December of each year.

*NON-ENTRY-LEVEL ASSOCIATE*

### Qualifications

**Quality of work:** Each associate is expected to have a solid grasp of various areas of law, including concepts, rules, and issues; draft all documents; and negotiate matters with some guidance.

**Quantity of work:** Each associate is expected to work 2,300 hours per year on behalf of the firm, 1,900 of which are billable and 400 of which are directed toward other firm-approved responsibilities. The senior lawyers and shareholders are responsible for providing sufficient files for an associate to meet this requirement.

*Client relations:* Each associate should take direct responsibility for solving client problems.

*New business development:* Each associate should participate in community activities and develop contacts and relationships for future business development.

*Personal qualities:* Each associate should serve as a resource for entry-level associates, exhibit good people skills, and comfortably handle a variety of situations.

*Tenure:* An entry-level associate generally qualifies for this position after three years of practice. It is anticipated that an associate will remain in this capacity for an additional three years before qualifying for further advancement.

### Compensation Potential:

Associate salaries currently range from $__,000 to $__,000, per annum. Salary progression is based on improved personal performance. Adjustments to salary are made annually, effective on the employee's anniversary date of employment with the firm.

In addition to salary, an associate may qualify for a bonus of up to ___ percent of annual salary. Bonuses are discretionary, based on both individual and firm performance, and are awarded during December of each year. An associate will be paid one-third of a bonus when it is awarded, one-third six months after the award, and one-third twelve months after the award. Deferred bonus payments require continued employment through the date of payment.

### SENIOR LAWYER

### Qualifications

*Quality of work:* Each senior lawyer should be reliable and versatile, with deep expertise enhanced by considerable experience, and have the ability to work independently with no significant professional guidance.

*Quantity of work:* Each senior lawyer is expected to work 2,400 hours per year on behalf of the firm, 1,900 of which are billable and 500 of which are directed toward development of business, practice management, and business management.

*Client relations:* Each senior lawyer should manage client relationships, and may be the chief client contact for a specific area of law.

*New business development:* Senior lawyers are expected to have more than enough client relationships to provide sufficient work for themselves and others.

*Personal qualities:* Each senior lawyer should have earned and should retain the respect, trust, and confidence of clients, shareholders, peers, and other personnel. Each senior lawyer should have the judgment and maturity to handle most problem situations without supervision.

*Tenure:* A lawyer generally becomes eligible for senior-lawyer status after six years of practice and two years as an associate of the firm. A senior lawyer is expected to spend at least three years as a senior lawyer of the firm to qualify for promotion to shareholder status. The firm does not have an "up or out" policy, and therefore progression to shareholder status may or may not occur.

### Compensation Potential

Senior lawyer salaries currently range from $___,000 to $___,000, per annum. Salary progression is based on improved personal performance. Adjustments to salary are made annually, effective on the employee's anniversary date of employment with the firm.

In addition to salary, a senior lawyer may qualify for a bonus of up to __ percent of annual salary. Bonuses are based on individual, team, and firm performance. Bonuses are awarded during December of each year. A senior lawyer will be paid one-third of a bonus when it is awarded, one-third nine months after the award, and one-third 18 months after the award. Deferred bonus payments require continued employment through the date of payment. Deferred bonus payments will be made if termination of employment is due to death or permanent disability.

### SHAREHOLDER

### Qualifications

*Quality of work:* A shareholder is expected to have achieved excellence in legal scholarship, expertise in broad practice areas, and the ability to solve complex problems.

*Quantity of work:* Each shareholder should commit 2,200 to 2,400 hours to the benefit of the firm, 1,500 to 1,700 of which are billable and 700 to 900 of which are devoted to management of the practice and firm and the development of business.

*Client relations:* A shareholder should act as a senior-level legal and business advisor to clients, and introduce clients—and transfer client working relationships—to other members of the firm.

*New business development:* A shareholder must manage and expand client relationships, and bring new clients and business into the firm, providing work for others.

*Personal qualities:* A shareholder must collaborate with other shareholders as well as other personnel, cooperate and support the common effort, effectively train and teach junior lawyers, and demonstrate a true spirit of "partnership." A shareholder must be stable, mature, and decisive, and exhibit superior judgment.

### Compensation Potential

Shareholder salaries currently begin at $\_\_\_,000, per annum. Bonuses may be awarded.

Career tracks and skill sets as the foundation of recruiting, evaluating, remunerating, and advancing associates have begun to take hold in the profession. Law firms are becoming acutely aware of the need to do a much better job at developing and retaining the right associates. To do this, one must look at more than compensation methodology and structure. Peter B. Sloan wrote about the journey and efforts of Blackwell Sanders Peper Martin LLP to move from associate lockstep to a more comprehensive associate career management process.[4] The book is a very quick and easy read. About two-thirds of its 107 pages are devoted to appendices that set forth the definitions, tools, matrices, and forms developed by the firm. This book is an important addition to this topic.

## Individual-Performance Salary Administration

The individual-performance salary administration system is probably the most difficult to design because of its lack of structure. Salary and bonus are no longer separate concepts; instead, compensation approaches a commission orientation, where the associate is paid a low salary plus a percentage of fees collected and business produced. The percentages may range from as low as 5 percent to as high as 50 percent. Smaller law firms are more likely to have such systems, as are plaintiff personal-injury practices. There are several reasons why this arrangement is often undesirable from the employer's point of view.

First, the clients that most junior associates can obtain are likely to be those that do not pay well. Because an associate is paid a salary to work on these matters, and receives a percentage of the gross as well, the economics of this system do not affect the associate but may adversely affect the employer. Using the earlier example, the firm cannot afford much of a commission without subsidizing the program. Most firms do not adjust the salary low enough to make such a proposition reasonable; therefore, they find themselves in the position of passing profits back down to the associates.

Second, when an associate receives premiums or commissions for bringing in clients, the associate typically gives priority to those personal clients rather than firm clients. This defeats the original purpose of hiring an associate, which almost invariably is because the firm has more work than it can handle. It also diverts the associate's productive energies from the generally more established and lucrative clients of the firm toward work of lesser quality. The law firm finds itself in the difficult position of establishing a reward system that requires an associate to reject much of the work as undesirable, and trying to maintain an incentive program designed to encourage client generation.

Such arrangements are, therefore, often not preferable because they tend to disregard the profitability of the work, the overhead required, or the desirability of such work for the firm. However, there are reasons to consider individual-performance salary plans. The firm can adopt a plan that advances an individual along a salary path that rewards established economic and client service performance. This can be done using either the years-of-experience or career-track salary administration method.

## Bonuses

Most law firms pay performance-based bonuses. Although most firms profess that their bonus structures are discretionary, the author's experience is that in operation, many of these plans are quite inflexible. In fact, most associates view bonuses as lump-sum salary payments that are deferred to year-end.

Firms with bonus plans sometimes pay low base salaries and compensate for that with consistently high year-end bonuses. Such a strategy is probably unwise in a market that competes based on salary more than compensation potential. Most junior lawyers compare salaries, not total earnings, when they get together to compare firms. Consequently, those firms that operate with such systems may reap competitive benefits by eliminating bonuses and raising salaries. Higher base pay may also be more highly valued by the associates, such that a $20,000 year-end bonus may be worth $15,000 in additional salary.

On the other hand, a discretionary-bonus arrangement can provide a control mechanism over labor costs and allow for immediate recognition of outstanding performance. In developing bonuses, firms consistently weigh several factors, including fees generated and clients produced. However, few firms reward only extraordinary individual performance or superlative firm achievement. In fact, 76 percent of senior associates are likely to get a bonus. When three out of four associates get a bonus, it is not because of extraordinary performance of either the individual or the firm. Such firms are either managing an effective variable pay program or simply handing out money.

One common incentive is the production-based bonus. When an associate can get a percentage of gross production over some minimum threshold, then the associate has an incentive to work hard. If the incentive is based on fees collected or billings, it prevents the associate from overworking files, but places the individual at the mercy of the billing partner who, if not constrained, may simply allocate all negative adjustments to the associate, regardless of merit. If the incentive is based on hours, there is the problem of overworking files to the detriment of the client. Carefully drafted rules for adjustments—and enforcement of the rules set forth—are necessary for effective operation of such systems. The partners, not the associates, should absorb the discount or premium of billing adjustments. Or, the adjustments should at least be based on relative time value among all timekeepers on a matter.

Another incentive system rewards associates by combining individual and firm performance factors with a numeric scoring system. One such plan is discussed below.

## Sample Associate Compensation Program

*SALARY*

Salary is based on market conditions, performance, service to the firm over time, years of experience, training, and day-to-day responsibilities. Different salary ranges exist for various levels of professional staff at the firm.

- Junior Associate        $\_\_\_,000 to $\_\_\_,000
- Associate               $\_\_\_,000 to $\_\_\_,000
- Senior Associate        $\_\_\_,000 to $\_\_\_,000
- Principal               $\_\_\_,000 to $\_\_\_,000

*BONUS*

### Philosophy

The bonus program provides the potential to earn additional compensation based on both individual and firm performance. In awarding bonuses, the firm will consider factors that cannot be readily measured. Such factors include efforts, assigned responsibilities for management, training, and the like. However, the lawyers must recognize that the primary criterion is the rendering of high-quality, timely, and cost-effective legal services on behalf of clients that are important to the short- and long-term success of the firm. These services must be of superior value and integrity and must be performed in an efficient manner, measured not just against alternatives, but also in absolute terms. While recognizing that the ideal is never achievable, the firm acknowledges that nothing less can be an acceptable goal. The foregoing must take place within an environment that permits high levels of personal satisfaction and achievement by all lawyers.

### Objectives

The incentive compensation system supports four basic organization objectives:

◆ Encouraging excellence in client service
◆ Encouraging teamwork
◆ Encouraging productivity
◆ Retaining talented employees
◆ Each objective facilitates achievement of the firm's goals. Following is a brief rationale for each objective.

*Encouraging excellence in client service:* Clients are the lifeblood of the business of law. Each member of the firm must know the firm's clients, understand their needs, and work diligently, effectively, and efficiently on their behalf.

*Encouraging teamwork:* The practice of law today is a complex endeavor that requires interdisciplinary efforts and coordination among lawyers, legal assistants, and administrative and support staff. Teamwork must be demonstrated among the members of the firm. The success of the individual is dependent upon the success of the firm as a whole.

*Encouraging productivity:* It is imperative that the resources of the firm are put to their highest and best use. Review of firm processes must occur with the objective of improving and streamlining those processes to ensure the most timely and cost-effective delivery of legal services possible. Efficiencies will ensure that (1) each employee's skills are utilized, (2) responsiveness is as rapid as possible, (3) duplication of effort is eliminated, (4) automation is used to enhance productivity, and (5) redundant and unnecessary work is eliminated.

*Retaining talented employees:* There is a significant cost associated with underutilized and discouraged employees: the loss of talented employees, and the need to replace their skills and knowledge of the law. It is incumbent upon the firm to ensure that employees are well treated and compensated appropriately and competitively. The firm's bonus program assists in that objective.

### Eligibility

The incentive plan will be prorated on an annual basis, and all lawyers will be eligible, with the following stipulations:

◆ Each new employee must have a minimum of six months of service
◆ Employees who retire or are ill during the calendar year will be eligible for the incentive plan on a prorated basis

### Bonus Pool

The firm shall establish a bonus savings fund in which it will deposit funds throughout the year. The size of the pool will likely change from year to year. Lawyers shall be kept informed of the size of the bonus fund.

### Criteria

*Fee production:* Fees produced—measured at the time of collection (cash receipts)—will be valued based on individual performance as a working lawyer and for the firm overall. The firm's goal will be measured on an average per full-time equivalent lawyer basis. Each lawyer shall have a goal for fee production for purposes of establishing the firm target.

| Individual fee production compared with individual goal | Individual points |
|---|---|
| greater than 20% unfavorable variance | 0.00 |
| 10% unfavorable variance to 20% unfavorable variance | 0.50 |
| 10% unfavorable variance to firm target | 1.50 |
| firm target to 10% favorable variance | 2.50 |
| 10% favorable variance to 20% favorable variance | 5.00 |
| greater than 20% favorable variance | 8.00 |

*Average profitability per file:* This is measured as the ratio of net fees produced (total paid to firm less direct costs of file as determined by firm's cost allocation system) to the total paid to the firm. Each lawyer and the firm's overall performance will be evaluated. The firm's goal will be based on a three-year historical average. Individuals will be evaluated against the firm goal. Individual points will be based on an overall average for the year.

| Individual file profitability ratio compared with firm goal | Individual points |
|---|---|
| greater than 20% unfavorable variance | 0.00 |
| 10% unfavorable variance to 20% unfavorable variance | 0.25 |
| 10% unfavorable variance to firm target | 0.75 |
| firm target to 10% favorable variance | 1.25 |
| 10% favorable variance to 20% favorable variance | 2.50 |
| greater than 20% favorable variance | 4.00 |

*Average turnaround per file:* This is measured in months from the date the file is received in the office until the client receives settlement or the matter is closed. Each lawyer and the firm's overall performance will be evaluated. The firm's goal will be based on a three-year historical average. Individuals will be evaluated against the firm goal.

| Individual average turnaround in months, compared with firm goal | Individual points |
|---|---|
| greater than 10% unfavorable variance | 0.00 |
| 10% unfavorable variance to firm target | 0.25 |
| firm target to 10% favorable variance | 0.50 |
| 10% favorable variance to 20% favorable variance | 1.20 |
| greater than 20% favorable variance | 2.40 |

*Subjective determination:* This will be established by the firm, based on a determination of effort, other accomplishments, seniority, and other factors deemed relevant. The firm can award anywhere from 0 to 1.6 points. The normal award would be .75 points.

### Calculation and Weighting

Bonuses will be calculated by assigning points to each of the criteria. For each criterion, firm performance will affect the final points an individual will accumulate.

| *Firm performance compared with target* | *Firm factor* |
|---|---|
| greater than 20% unfavorable variance | 0.00 |
| 10% unfavorable variance to 20% unfavorable variance | 0.25 |
| 10% unfavorable variance to firm target | 0.75 |
| firm target to 10% favorable variance | 1.00 |
| 10% favorable variance to 20% favorable variance | 1.10 |
| greater than 20% favorable variance | 1.25 |

Employee Points = Fee Production Points
+ File Profitability Points
+ Average Turnaround Points
+ Subjective Points

Weighted Firm Factor = [.60 x Firm Fee Production Factor]
+ [.30 x Firm File Profitability Factor]
× [.10 x Firm File Turnaround Factor]

Bonus = Employee Salary x Employee Points %
× Weighted Firm Factor

Under this plan, the maximum bonus would be 20 percent. This would require the highest individual and firm ratings for each criterion. A normal bonus under this plan, which assumes performance at target for individuals and firm, would be 5 percent.

## Example

*John's salary: $75,000*

John is at target on fee production, 10 percent below target for file productivity, and 20 percent favorable compared with file turnaround.

The firm is 20 percent above target on fee production, at target for file profitability, and 25 percent unfavorable for file turnaround.

The firm awards John 1.6 subjective points for practice management and associate training efforts.

*John's bonus:*

Employee points = 2.50 + 0.75 + 2.40 + 1.60
                        = 7.25

Firm factor       = (0.60 x 1.25) + (0.30 x 1.00) x (0.10 x 0.00)
                        = 0.75 + 0.30 + 0.00
                        = 1.05

Bonus              = $75,000 x 7.25% x 1.05
                        = $5,709

The key to successful implementation of an incentive program such as the one just described is to select only three or four critical factors to measure. At least one factor should be subjectively awarded to balance objective criteria.

## Timing of Bonus Payment

Production-based incentives are often paid monthly or quarterly. Although this incentive rewards the individual almost immediately, it can create problems for the employer. First, there is the potential for manipulation of work to boost short-term performance and achieve or increase the bonus. The consequence is that the following period's performance may not meet expectations. Adjustments or subsidiary bookkeeping can mitigate this, but with additional administrative burdens. Second, paying bonuses periodically under such a scheme results in additional payroll complexities. Ideally, the payroll should be a nonevent once it is established at the beginning of the year. Bonuses can be just as rewarding when paid at year-end, with less bookkeeping and payroll disruption.

## Endnotes

1. *Survey of Law Firm Economics* (Newtown Square, PA: Altman Weil Publications, Inc., 2003), 166.

2. Clara N. Carson, *The Lawyer Statistical Report: The US Legal Profession in 1995* (ABA Bar Foundation, 1999), 4, 6.

3. *Survey of Law Firm Economics* (Newtown Square, PA: Altman Weil Publications, Inc., 2003).

4. Peter B. Sloan, *From Classes to Competencies, Lockstep to Levels: How One Law Firm Discarded Lockstep Associate Advancement and Replaced It with an Associate Level System* (Blackwell Sanders Peper Martin, LLP, 2002).

# *Paraprofessional Compensation*

**4**

## Overview

The attributes of compensating paralegal assistants are similar to those for associate lawyers, as described in the previous chapter. However, paralegal compensation does not have the elements of business generation or advancement to ownership. Also, the dollars involved in the compensation decisions are less.

A significant issue regarding paralegal compensation is whether an individual is "exempt" or "nonexempt" under the wage and hour laws of the Fair Labor Standards Act (FLSA). Unfortunately, there is no clear answer. The exempt or nonexempt determination depends on the facts and circumstances of the positions within a firm; it could even be that both exempt and nonexempt paralegal assistant positions exist within a firm. The issue is an important one, as it affects the payment of overtime compensation and other human resource issues. Appendix 4 sets forth general specifications regarding exemption. The following guidelines, which provide assistance in connection with paralegals, are not determinative—each firm must conduct an appropriate review of case and statutory law. Expert assistance is recommended.

## Paralegal Classifications

Paralegal assistants historically qualified for an exempt position as either a professional or administrative employee. A review of each classification follows. See Appendix 4 for the status of exempt classifications and a chart comparing current and proposed changes to the regulation.

### Professional (under current law as of September 2003)

The most difficult test for classification as a professional employee is whether the position's primary duties require advanced knowledge customarily acquired through advanced instruction. It has been Altman Weil's experience that similar positions have not met this test, even though they require extensive educational training. To compound the difficulty, only 20 percent of the individual's time can be devoted to nonprofessional duties. Given this narrow definition and interpretation, it may be unlikely that a paralegal position would be granted an exemption as a professional employee.

### Administrative (under current law as of September 2003)

To be classified as an administrative employee, the primary job duties must involve office and nonmanual work relating to the management and operations of the employer. Further, an administrative employee must customarily exercise discretion and independent judgment, require only general supervision, assist an executive, and perform job duties requiring special skills. These definitions could be satisfied by many paralegals. The other requirements for nonexempt work and salary will most likely be met, but cannot be overlooked.

### Making the Determination

Each firm must decide for itself whether a paralegal assistant is qualified for an exemption and whether the firm wants to face the possibility of justifying its position. Page & Addison, P.C., a small Dallas law firm, was successful in defending its paralegals as exempt administrative employees in a U.S. Department of Labor lawsuit. See *Robert B. Reich, Secretary of Labor, U.S. Department of Labor v. Page & Addison, P.C.*, No. 3; 91-CV-2655-P, (Northern District of Texas, March 10, 1994). A *Wall Street Journal* article summarizes the varied issues and interests in the classification of paralegals as exempt or nonexempt.[1] Information collected by the Association of Legal Administrators in one of its national annual surveys indicates that 68 percent of respondents classified paralegals solely as nonexempt personnel.[2] Twelve percent of the respondents indicated that they use both exempt and nonexempt classifications for their paralegal employees (four times the level reported in their 1999 study); 20 percent of the respondents indicated that they classified paralegals as exempt.[3] Law firm participants dominated the study.

## Paralegal Compensation

Because paralegals are fee producers, their compensation can be heavily influenced by the production of fee revenues. In evaluating paralegals, firms must be comfortable using fee-earner data; that is, a standard means of allocating overhead among all fee earners (partners, associates, and paralegals). The generally accepted standard is that one lawyer equals two paralegal assistants, which equals one fee earner. Therefore, a law firm with ten lawyers and five paralegal assistants has twelve and one-half fee earners. This is the standard definition used in most surveys. Table 4.1 depicts an average paralegal's economic performance, using that standard definition. As you can see, at the survey's average, paralegals are profitable. This is a significant improvement over prior studies, largely attributable to increased billing rates. This study, of course, does not consider nonbillable or noncshargeable contributions that are a portion of a paralegal's duties. Paralegals are generally expected to be working on billable matters 72.6 percent of their total work hours.[4]

Individual firms may develop other means of allocation. Altman Weil has seen rational systems that treat a paralegal as one-quarter to three-fourths of a fee earner. Some firms even allocate differently among the lawyers. Each firm must look to its own data and use of resources, balanced against some measure of simplicity and ease of calculation. Paralegal compensation can then be structured much like associate compensation. It is preferable to establish consistent reward strategies across the organization. This simplifies

**TABLE 4.1**
**Profitability of Paralegals**

|  | Paralegals as a Group* | Paralegals as a Percentage of Associates |
|---|---|---|
| **Fee production** |  |  |
| Average annual billable hours | 1,397 | 75.8% |
| Average standard billing rate | $ 114 | 64.4% |
| Fee production | $159,258 | 48.8% |
| Average time written off | $(8,918) | 48.8% |
| Billable fees produced | $150,340 |  |
| Average AR written off | $(5,262) |  |
| **Position costs** |  |  |
| Cash receipts | $145,078 |  |
| Average overhead | $ 60,982 | 50.0% |
| Average total compensation | $ 56,733 | 48.7% |
| Position cost | $117,715 |  |
| **Profitability** |  |  |
| Cash basis profit (loss) | $ 27,363 |  |
| Cash basis margin | 17.2% |  |

NOTES:
1. Average overhead includes all firm expenses, except lawyer and paralegal compensation.
2. Total compensation includes cash, benefits, retirement contributions, and employer taxes.
*Source: *2002 Annual Compensation Survey for Legal Assistants/Paralegals and Managers* (Newtown Square, PA: Altman Weil Publications, Inc., 2002).

administrative matters and creates alignment among employees regarding the activities that are important to success.

Unfortunately, as can be seen from the above example, paralegal utilization is only about 76 percent of the average associate. The reasons for this are many and varied, though it usually says more about lawyers' willingness to use paralegals than anything else. Clients, the firm, and the paralegals all have economic interests in improving utilization.

Because paralegal utilization lags and is often outside the control of the individual, compensation structures must not penalize the individual for results that are failings of the system or of the firm. Paralegal time is often hit the hardest when write-offs are taken on a matter. Paralegals sit on the lowest rung of the fee-producer ladder, with far more limited career opportunities than the lawyers. The rationale often goes like this: "It won't hurt the paralegals' careers or their incomes." That attitude may prevail even in a firm that pays paralegals bonuses based on fee generation. (Eighty-two percent of paralegals qualify for bonus consideration in their law firms; discretionary systems comprise three-quarters of paralegal bonus programs, while formulaic awards comprise just over one-fifth of such programs.)

However, paralegals may not be hired primarily for billable work. In those instances, their compensation structure must reflect the relative value of the position's duties and responsibilities. See chapter 5 for a discussion of such systems.

It is important to establish an appropriate psychological environment among all fee producers so that personal income opportunities are not artificially diminished. This extends beyond billing, to staffing and task assignments.

It may be appropriate in certain situations to grant fictitious fee credits for continuing legal education, accounting tasks, bar activities, pro bono work, and the like. Such assignments may be more cost effective for the firm if handled by paralegals. Accordingly, compensation should recognize such value.

Paralegals assigned to high-risk or contingent matters should share in the allocation of premiums to compensate for their work on those matters where no fee is earned.

Paralegal compensation varies by location, size of firm, and other factors. Tables 4.2 and 4.3 provide a sample of such variability.

## Endnotes

1. Andrew Gerlin, "Firm's Paralegals Can Be Exempt from Overtime Pay, Jury Decides," *Wall Street Journal*, March 16, 1994.

2. *2002 Compensation and Benefits Survey* (Lincolnshire, IL: Association of Legal Administrators, September 2002), 10.

3. Ibid.

4. Ibid., 18.

**TABLE 4.2**
**Selected Paralegal Compensation Data**

|  | *Lower Quartile* *(Legal Assistant)** |
| --- | --- |
| East South Central† | $34,506 |
| New England | $43,175 |
| 3 to 5 years of experience | $37,315 |
| 16 to 20 years of experience | $44,102 |
| Under 20 lawyers | $30,173 |
| 100 to 399 lawyers | $40,000 |
| No specialty | $32,129 |
| IP | $44,439 |

*Amounts represent total cash compensation.
†Kentucky, Tennessee, Mississippi, and Alabama.

Source: *2002 Annual Compensation Survey for Legal Assistants/Paralegals and Managers* (Newtown Square, PA: Altman Weil Publications, Inc., 2002).

**TABLE 4.3**
**Selected Paralegal Compensation Data**

|  | *Ninth decile* *(Working Manager/Supervisor)** |
| --- | --- |
| Middle Atlantic Region | $132,514 |
| 11 to 15 years of experience | $110,092 |
| 400 and over lawyers | $132,514 |
| Litigation | $103,581 |

*Amounts represent total cash compensation.

Source: *2002 Annual Compensation Survey for Legal Assistants/Paralegals and Managers* (Newtown Square, PA: Altman Weil Publications, Inc., 2002).

# Staff Compensation

**5**

## Overview

As the number of lawyers employed by firms has grown, so has the number of staff persons who support them. Law firm support staffs used to be small and consist predominately of hourly employees. Such individuals were primarily concerned with their hourly rates or weekly take-home pay. Little sophistication was required in administration of their compensation structure.

Larger firms today employ a significant number of professional, semiprofessional, and managerial employees who are not covered by the overtime requirements of the labor laws. Although these employees may have compensation structures that are similar to those for hourly employees, they expect—and tend to have—higher salary, enhanced benefit packages, and bonus programs that are tied to individual and group performance.

The Fair Labor Standards Act (FLSA) covers many non-lawyer staff persons. That means that the employer must meet minimum wage standards and comply with the overtime pay provisions of that act. Only employees whose job *functions* meet the specific FLSA requirements are exempt. See Appendix 4 for a summary of the exemptions to FLSA overtime requirements.

## Setting Wage Scales

There are two comprehensive sources of wage data, available for many cities and some regions:

1. The U.S. Department of Labor Bureau of Labor Statistics conducts metropolitan area studies that contain compensation information, by industry and size of employer (**http://stats.bls.gov**).

2. The Association of Legal Administrators (**http://www.alanet.org**— look under Products, then Financial Management, then scroll down to the Survey), conducts surveys of the compensation of twenty-five nonlawyer administrative positions. Information is provided by type of organization, size of organization, geographic location (region, state, metropolitan area), experience, education, certification, and supervisory responsibility. Data for means, medians, and first and third quartiles are provided when possible. Each position is defined in the study. Note that local chapters often conduct their own surveys as well.

Every job has a minimum value. You simply cannot find people who have the necessary skills and will take the job (and stay for any length of time) for less than that minimum amount. If you refer to local surveys, the first-quartile amount (twenty-fifth percentile) will generally be near the minimum you would pay in a law office. Employees in the lowest-paid quartile are not likely to meet law office standards of skill and performance.

The third quartile (seventy-fifth percentile) of wages in the local market may be your upper limit, with a few exceptions. Every job has a maximum worth. To illustrate, a secretary is usually paid less than a lawyer—even a new lawyer—in today's market. Also, a good legal secretary is generally paid more than a receptionist. This market-driven hierarchy of jobs sets upper limits, as does the employer's desire to limit labor costs.

In its booklet, *Guide for Evaluating Your Firm's Jobs and Pay,* the Bureau of Labor Statistics describes its methodology (generic leveling) for evaluating jobs in its compensation surveys.[1] Each selected occupation is classified into one of several work levels, based on duties and responsibilities. The process of determining the work level of an occupation is called generic leveling. It is generic because it is designed to determine the work level of nearly all occupations found in the economy. The work level of the occupation is determined by using ten factors, each of which is broken down into a number of levels. Each level has a written description and a fixed number of points. The ten factors are as follows:

1. Knowledge
2. Supervision received
3. Guidelines
4. Complexity
5. Scope and effect
6. Personal contacts

7. Purpose of contacts
8. Physical demands
9. Work environment
10. Supervisory duties

The total amount of points from all generic leveling factors determines an employee's work level. This tool is an excellent aid for matching an employer's positions with comparable positions in the surveys. Job titles can be misleading; comparable duties and responsibilities provide much better reference points. The resource also aids in properly aligning wage scales among positions.

## Salary Increases

Salary review, especially in smaller law offices, has many political facets. For example, lawyers may want to procure pay increases for their personal secretaries to assuage their own egos or to ensure that they (the lawyers) receive maximum support. The result may be interpartner warfare, and staff compensation that is based on "boss power" rather than on notions of equity or value to the firm.

Any system designed to compensate people is subject to abuse, of course, even when administered centrally through a personnel committee or an administrator rather than through the dictates of individual partners. But, in general, when one manager or a small committee undertakes a salary review process, there is a better chance that the process will be impartial and benefit both employer and employees.

In small law firms, the process of handing out raises will generally be (and should be) relatively informal. There may be no need to do more than carefully consider each employee's contributions—as part of a regular performance review process—and deal with the topic once a year. However, the results must be fully and carefully communicated to individual employees, even when the determination is made informally.

Larger organizations need a more formal program, because an individual manager or a small committee cannot judge the performance and value of a large number of people without the benefit of a system. In a larger firm, the development of detailed, specific procedures and the implementation of an evaluation system can most effectively be handled by a trained, experienced human-resources manager.

### Performance Appraisal and Salary Review

Through the performance appraisal process, each employee should know what the firm expects in job performance. The best way to develop an understanding of these expectations is through the use of job competency models. Competencies include the education, experience, skills, and knowledge required for a job. A competency model organizes the competencies into broad categories, such as personal attributes, leadership qualities, functional expertise, and the like. Each category has underlying competencies. For example, the category of leadership qualities might have underlying competencies of negotiating, problem solving, coaching, and the like. Each competency is assigned both required and desired proficiency levels, such as basic, intermediate, advanced, and mastery.

This approach differs from the traditional job description, which sets forth job functions as well as minimum requirements for education and experience. Often the latter are shown in combination with trade-offs (for example, more direct experience offsetting less education). A written job description usually has the following layout: the job title, education and experience requirements, primary duties, reporting relationships (up and down) and coworker relationships (team assignments, both intergroup and intragroup), wage scale, and FLSA classification. Other matters—such as what is expected regarding attendance, overtime work, willingness to assist other employees who may be overburdened, and the like—should be covered in the employee manual, but are often repeated in job descriptions. Sometimes a job description bears little resemblance to the actual job being performed, because a job often changes in character over time. Typically, little effort is made to inculcate such changes into the evaluation and performance development processes.

The competency model is performance based. By assessing an individual's competency inventory, it is possible to determine development initiatives and profile the individual against possible job openings. Further, because competencies are performance based, the employer and employee can focus on changes occurring in the job, and the competencies being acquired by the employee.

Informal performance appraisals should take place on a continuing basis. The best time to say thank you or to correct a problem is when the situation arises, or very shortly thereafter. Frequent, open, and constructive communication between employees and supervisors goes a long way toward fostering good performance. As another consequence, employees will generally not be surprised when formal evaluations are delivered.

Following are some guidelines for supervisors in conducting evaluation discussions with employees:

- Allow enough time to have a full discussion without interruption.
- Reduce tension by encouraging the employee to sit comfortably in your office, or, even better, in a neutral conference room.

- ◆ Maintain eye contact and listen carefully to be sure that the employee understands.
- ◆ Focus on proficiencies and deficiencies in the performance of the job, not on personality traits.
- ◆ Be sure to include strengths, as well as weaknesses, in your discussion, but do not give the wrong impression if the overall rating is unsatisfactory.
- ◆ Encourage a discussion of how the employee can improve performance. Emphasize the future.
- ◆ Be prepared to acknowledge disagreements, but make sure the employee understands that the firm expects him or her to perform according to certain standards.
- ◆ At the end of the session, agree to an action plan with specific milestones and timelines. Each employee has strengths and weaknesses. The action plan should set forth what needs to be done to preserve and enhance strengths and to mitigate weaknesses. It should be prioritized, recognizing that the employee cannot do everything at once. It is better to pick the most crucial two or three competencies and focus on them. Each action plan should contain at least one strength for further enhancement.

Review procedures should be incorporated in the firm's office manual, and should be discussed with new employees at initial orientation sessions. This ensures that new employees understand the firm's evaluation process and salary program, and that evaluation aids employees in their work.

Most firms should conduct initial reviews of new employees after their first three to six months of employment, and thereafter on either their anniversary dates of employment or a standard date each year. For example, a firm might review all nonexempt staff during the second quarter of the year, with pay adjustments taking effect on July 1, and all exempt personnel during the fourth quarter, with pay adjustments taking effect on January 1. The advantage to such a program is that all personnel performance is captured at the same time and all pay adjustments are internally consistent relative to performance. Using the anniversary date makes it possible for evaluations to occur throughout the year, thus relieving the pressure to do all reviews at once. However, pay adjustments that occur on anniversary dates complicate the processes of budgeting and managing internal equity. Salary adjustments, therefore, should generally be made once each year. A firm must be careful in this instance that the pay message, which may occur several months after the evaluation, is not inconsistent (good or bad) with the individual's current performance. Some employers make a pay adjustment if the employee successfully completes the initial three-to-six-month introductory period.

The manager of human resources has the responsibility of (1) determining the personnel involved in each of the firm's various groups, (2) contacting all appropriate raters, and (3) collecting evaluation forms from all raters. The manager should review each form to ensure that a fair, objective evaluation has been given. Lawyers and other supervisors who are deficient or ineffective in giving written evaluations should be counseled. In addition, all lawyers and staff involved with the evaluation process should be aware of pertinent federal and state laws covering employment issues. Improper comments, either written or verbal, can impede improved employee performance and result in negative legal consequences for the employer. Firms may want to consider having in-service training sessions on the topic of evaluation skills, conducted by human resources professionals or employment counsel. After all forms have been completed and reviewed, the office manager or personnel manager or supervisor should conduct a private evaluation conference with each rated employee.

Computer-scoring systems exist for performance appraisals. Such systems can—with speed, efficiency, and useful analysis—help form a comprehensive evaluation and comparative assessment process. The analysis not only compares employees across the specific performance metrics evaluated, it also assesses the objectivity of individual raters. This final step is important in making the process truly objective and valid.

Through other administrative systems, employers should collect separate, objective records on each employee's performance. For example, sign-in and sign-out sheets and time records can be used to monitor employee attendance, and production and accuracy records may be considered in word processing and other areas where electronic records of performance may be compiled. Also, supervisors can comment on the cooperation of secretaries in accepting overflow work.

In many law offices, it is not appropriate for only the employee's immediate supervisor to complete evaluation forms. Typically, lawyers work together on projects, and secretaries help one another to get the work done. Thus, lawyers have contact with several secretaries and can participate in the evaluation process for each of them. There is often less crossover of work among support groups such as file clerks and word processors, so their only evaluators may be support department supervisors.

The concept of a "360-degree evaluation," largely accepted in corporate America, has not been widely embraced by law firms. Nevertheless, some prefer such an approach because it reflects the reality of the modern workplace. Each individual's performance affects superiors, coworkers, subordinates, and clients. Designing an appraisal system that solicits input from each of the groups yields a better knowledge base regarding an individual's performance.

Also, individuals should rate their own performance. How we see ourselves can be just as important as how others see us.

## Bonuses

Both nonexempt personnel (76 percent) and exempt personnel (84 percent) qualify for bonus consideration in their law firms. The programs are overwhlemingly discretionary (as opposed to fixed percentages, fixed dollar amounts, or formulas) in setting award amounts.

The bonus portion of cash compensation is the variable component—at least it should be. Often a bonus is considered nothing more than deferred salary or "that extra check we get at year-end." In labor-intensive businesses, variable pay exists to make it easier to adjust cost structures to changing revenue levels without the disruptive need to lay off employees. For this concept to work, there are certain conditions that must be met.

First, employees must actually view a bonus program as variable pay; that is, bonuses are earned when individual and organizational performance meets and exceeds certain performance and fiscal targets. Just putting in the time is not sufficient.

Second, a variable-pay program must share risks, as well as rewards. Employees may make less in times of poor economic performance and more in times of prosperity. These systems are often installed in dire times and then taken away when the economy recovers. The sharing of the rewards in good times might mean that a firm's employees are paid above market. That is okay, because everyone gains in that situation if it is done within a true variable-pay program.

Salary scales in variable-pay programs may be positioned lower in the market because of the upside opportunity in the bonus component. However, variable-pay programs still need salary scales sufficient to attract and retain the right employees—even in years when performance and fiscal results do not provide for bonus awards. Striking the balance between a sufficient base wage, the amount of bonus opportunity and consideration of risk is an exercise where expert guidance is recommended.

## Nonexempt Staff

Personnel policies for a law office's nonexempt staff must be based on consideration of the reasons this group of people works. The objectives and motivation of staff are sometimes different from those of lawyers or managers. Consider these factors:

- Staff employees are as likely to be secondary wage earners (supplementing family income) as primary wage earners.
- Many employees have major responsibilities for children or elders, and lack the economic resources to provide for alternate assistance.
- These occupations have shorter training periods than those for professional or management positions, and also have shorter on-the-job learning curves.
- There are few opportunities for advancement on the staff of a law office. While an associate lawyer may have a goal of becoming a partner, a secretary has little to achieve by way of advancement. Immediate reward is, therefore, more important.
- An important part of compensation is psychological rather than monetary. Being useful, needed, and appreciated is important to staff persons (as it is for all individuals).

Staff employees are generally hired from a local labor market. Secretaries or file clerks will rarely travel outside their local communities or metropolitan areas to work, and are much less likely to relocate to obtain new jobs. Consequently, the prevailing wage patterns that are important in fixing and comparing salary scales are those in the immediate locality. Because staff personnel can generally move between industries, wage patterns in all types of offices are pertinent to the compensation scale for a law office's staff. There are several sources of local wage information. In many cities, private-employer groups collect and disseminate such data. The local Chamber of Commerce, the state employment service, and the local chapter of the Association of Legal Administrators may also know of such sources.

# Exempt Staff

Managerial, technical, and professional positions are treated separately from hourly positions. Some of this distinction arises from different treatment under FLSA. Other differences arise because of the educational backgrounds required, the length of time it takes to become proficient at the job, the general level of supervision required, and the like. Unfortunately, many law firms have not fully integrated their burgeoning middle-management positions into their overall job value systems. They recognize that these individuals fall somewhere between the hourly staff and the lawyers.

## Senior Management

Providing some structure to senior-management positions begins by first segregating senior management from middle management. Senior managers are characterized by the closeness with which they work with owners. These individuals immerse themselves in positions in such a way that it can be difficult to separate the person from the position. Senior managers deal with stewardship of the owners' interests (which, at least in the District of Columbia, may include their own interests), and with strategic decisions as opposed to operational decisions. Senior managers have mostly exempt personnel reporting to them. Performance measurements tend to be structured around overall firm performance (that is, growth in partner income) and control and efficiency of nonlegal operations (overhead per fee earner, staffing ratios, satisfaction surveys, and the like).

At the senior-management level, age and length of service tend to have very little correlation with compensation. However, an organization's size is very much considered. In very small law firms, senior-management functions are often viewed as the responsibility of each partner, operating as a committee of the whole. As a firm grows, it may assign these functions to a managing partner or an executive committee. Only in the larger law firms do separate senior nonlawyer executives exist. Note that office managers in many firms do not function at the senior-management level, even though they may well be the most highly compensated nonlawyer administrative employees in those firms.

The labor market for senior management is certainly national in scope. National wage data, adjusted to local conditions, is critical for determining the prevailing levels of compensation. However, in law firms there is an executive compensation flash point. Unlike publicly traded companies where executives can earn nearly unlimited sums of money if performance warrants and the plans are established as such (we will not debate here whether such compensation plans really do pay for performance), executives in law firms face a compensation ceiling of average partner compensation levels. It would be rare indeed to find a nonlawyer CEO of a law firm earning consistently more than the average partner in the firm (see Illustration 5.1 for the relative compensation of nonlawyer CEOs and partners). Accordingly, it is less likely that there will be a formal salary range for the position.

## Middle Management

Today, middle management may be better defined as professional management. Due to a flat and lean organization attitude in many firms, middle management suffered the brunt of the early 1990s restructuring. Middle management still exists today, but it is often populated with professionally credentialed nonlawyers. Finance, human resources, risk management, marketing, and technology departments all have individuals with special credentials, such as state-certified licenses or association certifications. These indi-

**ILL. 5.1**

**Relative Average Compensation in Firms With 100 or More Lawyers**

Index

| | |
|---|---|
| 150 | |
| 100 | |
| 50 | |
| 0 | |

Lowest paid partner — CEO — Average partner — Managing partner — Highest paid partner

Source: 1997 and 2002 *Law Firm Managing Partner and Executive Director Survey*, Altman Weil® Publications, Inc., Newtown Square, PA 19073.

viduals have very specialized skills and experience. They are as likely to work independently as they are to work in teams or to supervise others.

Wage scales are set in different markets, reflecting the relative supply and demand for specific credentials as well as the other competencies that contribute to the hiring and compensation processes. The markets for these professional middle-management positions can vary. Accordingly, pay is industry-market driven and advances are based on productivity and contribution to a firm's mission. Perhaps the best conceptualization is a sense that the firm is a client of the middle manager, not just an employer.

### Supervisors

This is the entry level of the exempt group, or the most senior level of the nonexempt group. Pay considerations are usually strongly correlated with those of the subordinates supervised. One problem with supervisory positions is that they rarely contribute directly to profits (a fact well known by the supervisors). Another problem is that supervisors cannot control much of the outcome of their subordinates' efforts. Their training ground is in the subordinate positions they supervise.

These positions are defined and assigned pay levels in the same traditional manner as the nonexempt positions discussed earlier. Supervisors share the same local market, and, in most firms, will represent an internal promotion for an existing subordinate.

# Conclusion

Careful planning is required to pay staff personnel the right amount and to communicate pay decisions properly. Firms that do not attend to the process may pay too little, which can result in the loss of valuable talent. Rarely do firms pay too much. Making any plan a reality requires that people work in a focused and collaborative way. Typically, very little is gained by being cheap with talent. Paying employees well returns far more than what firms save by not doing so.

## Endnote

1. U.S. Department of Labor Bureau of Labor Statistics, *Guide for Evaluating Your Firm's Jobs and Pay* (October 1996), 3–5.

# One Firm's Rules for Allocation of Client Production Credit

## Underlying Premises

1. The long-followed concept that remuneration should be provided for the function of causing clients to patronize the firm is sound and fair, and should be continued.

2. The total amount of such remuneration is not dealt with herein. See firm's "Income Division Plan."

3. Basic to various of the firm's policies and practices are the concepts that no client is an individual firm member's client, but every client is the firm's client, and that, as between the firm and a client, all work performed for the client is performed by the firm and not by one or more particular firm members. It is, therefore, logical that to the extent that work performed for one client results in the engagement of the firm by another client who is not a "related client" (hereinafter defined), the new client ought to be deemed to have been originated at least in part by the partners.

4. When a new client comes to the firm not because of a connection with one or more particular firm members, and his or her advent is not known to be related to the firm's work for a prior client or some other similar factor,

all of the past practice of the partners as a group ought to be deemed to be the cause of the advent of such new client.

5. After a number of years of regular repeated service to a client, responsibility for such client's continuing to patronize the firm becomes blurred. In such case, it is logical to reward the income-sharing firm members (as a group) with part of the originators' share of the fees paid by such clients, on the theory that their work in prior years is in substantial measure responsible for the continued patronage.

6. Any scheme of income division ought to furnish a financial incentive to each firm member to try to see to it that each client's work is performed by whichever firm members can, all things considered, most efficiently perform it. Accordingly, and as a limitation on paragraph 5, above, the initial originators of a client should always continue to receive a portion of the originators' share of the fees paid by such client, subject to the consideration that it is impractical to account for minor fractions of a share.

## Rules

**Part A.** *General Rules.* Every firm member who has a substantial known connection with the advent of a new client shall be entitled to an aliquot part of the total originating credits provided in the firm's Income Division Plan for fees paid by such new client. If one or more firm members and the firm have a substantial connection with the advent of a new client, each such firm member and the partners as a group, shall be entitled to an aliquot part of the aforesaid originating credits. If no firm member is known to have a substantial connection with the advent of a new client, the partners as a group shall be entitled to all of the aforesaid originating credits.

> **Rule A-1.** *Definition of Firm Members.* "Firm member," as used in these rules, encompasses those persons who are partners or associates of the firm.
>
> **Rule A-2.** *Division of Originating Credits among Partners.* Originating credits allocable to partners as a group shall be divided among the individual partners as is provided in the firm's Income Division Plan.
>
> **Rule A-3.** *Definition of New Clients.* "New client," as used in these rules, will, absent compelling reasons otherwise, be deemed to encompass not only the individual who contacts a firm member for legal services, but all other individuals with like interests that the firm comes to represent with respect to the legal matter for which services are first sought by such individual. When it clearly appears that a former client for whom legal services have not been performed for a substantial period of time comes

to a firm member for new legal services for reasons clearly unrelated to the prior representation or work associations with firm members, the client shall be deemed a new client.

**Part B.** *Rules Applicable to Work-Oriented, Referral-Oriented, and Supplier-Oriented New Clients.* The rules of this Part B rather than the rules of Part A, above, shall determine who is entitled to receive the originating credits for work-oriented, referral-oriented, and supplier-oriented new clients.

**Rule B-1.** *Work-Oriented New Clients.* A work-oriented new client is either (1) one who initially became acquainted with the firm or a firm member by being directly exposed to prior work performed by the firm for another client or other clients, or (2) one who is referred either to the firm or a firm member by a person who has thus become acquainted with either the firm or that firm member.

Each of the following categories of firm members shall be entitled to an aliquot part of the total originating credits for fees paid by such new client: (a) the partners; (b) the firm members (including, if applicable, the partners as a group) who are, or before the application of the continuing-client rule (Part E) were, entitled to the originating credits for the prior work hereinabove referred to; (c) the firm member whom the new client asks to handle his or her first problem (see Rule B-6); and (d) any firm members who have a substantial connection with the advent of the new client that does not stem from any factor dealt with in Rules B-1, B-2, or B-3. If the prior work referred to in the first sentence of this Rule B-1 was performed for two or more clients, and there were two or more individual originators of them, none of whom was clearly dominant, category (b) above shall comprise the partners (and for this purpose, two or more related clients—see Part C—are deemed to be a single client). However, if in such case one of such individual originators was clearly dominant, then category (b) shall comprise him or her alone. (Regarding employments and referrals by "ABC" bank trust officers, see Rule B-9.)

**Rule B-2.** *Referral-Oriented New Clients.* "Referral," as used in this caption, does not relate to the referral of a client to the firm by someone else. It relates, rather, to a firm member's referring a client to a third person, to become that third person's customer or patient or client. Further, it relates only to a situation in which such referral by a firm member was made in connection with the rendition of the firm's professional service to that client. A referral-oriented new client is (1) one who has sold goods or services to one or more prior clients referred to him or her for such purchase by a firm member, or (2) one referred to the firm by such a seller of goods or services, but only when there appears to be a substantial inducing relationship between the aforesaid referral by a firm member and the advent of the new client. Each of the following categories of firm members shall be entitled to an aliquot part of the total originating credits for fees paid by such new client: (a) the partners, and (b) any firm members who have a substantial connection with the advent of the new client that does not stem from any factor dealt with in Rule B-1, B-2, or B-3. When there is no one in category (b), the entire originating credits shall be allotted to the partners.

**Rule B-3.** *Supplier-Oriented New Clients.* A supplier-oriented new client is (1) one who has sold goods or services to the firm, or (2) one referred to the firm by such a seller. The total originating credits for fees paid by any such new client shall be allocated as prescribed in Rule B-2.

**Rule B-4.** *Interaction of Rules B-1 and B-2, and of B-1 and B-3.* If factors exist that call for the application of Rule B-1 and also either Rule B-2 or Rule B-3:

**(1)** Rule B-1 alone shall control if the B-1 factor is the dominant one.

**(2)** Rule B-2 or Rule B-3 alone shall control if the B-2 or B-3 factor is the dominant one.

**(3)** If neither of the aforesaid factors is dominant, Rule B-1 shall control, but category (b) of that rule shall be deemed to comprise the partners.

**Rule B-5.** *Overriding Influence of Independent Factor.* If a factor calling for the application of Rule B-1, B-2, or B-3 exists, but at least one firm member has such a strong independent connection with the advent of a new client as to make it probable that he or she would have patronized the firm even if such factor did not exist, Rule B-1, B-2, or B-3, as the case may be, shall not be applied. Originating credits for fees paid by such new client shall be allotted pursuant to the provisions of Part A.

**Rule B-6.** *Fortuitous Events.* If a new client consults the firm and fortuitously ends up in the hands of a particular firm member, the partners shall be entitled to the aliquot part of the originating credits for fees paid by such new client that is allotted under Rule B-1 to the firm member whom a new client asks to handle his or her first problem. If a new client initially seeks one firm member and fortuitously ends up in the hands of another firm member, the firm member initially sought, and not the other firm member, shall be entitled to the aliquot part of the originating credits for fees paid by such new client that is allotted under Rule B-1 to the firm member whom a new client asked to handle his or her first problem.

**Rule B-7.** *Division of Aliquot Parts of Originating Credits among Firm Members.* Any aliquot part of originating credits that is allotted to the partners in this Part B shall be divided among individual partners as is provided in the firm's Income Division Plan. Any aliquot part of originating credits that is allotted to two or more firm members in category (b) of Rule B-1 shall be divided among those firm members in the same manner as are the originating credits for fees paid by the client for whom the prior work was performed that led to the advent of the new client. Any aliquot part of originating credits that is allotted to two or more firm members in category (d) of Rule B-1 or category (b) of Rule B-2 or Rule B-3 shall be divided among those firm members equally.

**Rule B-8.** *Employments and Referrals by "ABC" Bank Trust Officers.* Every new client who is a trust officer of "ABC" Bank, or who is referred by such a trust officer, is conclusively deemed to be "work-oriented." The originating credits for fees paid by such client shall be allotted one-third to the firm member, if any, whom the new client asks to handle his or her first problem, and the remaining two-thirds or three-thirds (if no individual firm members) to the partners. This Rule B-8 constitutes, principally, an application of Rule B-1, but it overrides every provision of these rules that is inconsistent herewith, except Rules B-5 and B-6 and Part E.

**Part C.** *Rules Applicable to Related Clients.* Notwithstanding the provisions of Parts A and B, above, originating credits for fees paid by a "related client" shall be divided among individual firm members in the same manner as are the originating credits for the client to whom such related client is related, unless it is clearly apparent that some factor other than the relationship between the prior client and the new client was the dominant factor in the latter's advent.

**Rule C-1.** *Definition of Related Client.* A client is related to another client when the one is (a) the personal representative of the other, (b) the trustee of a trust of which the other is trustor, (c) the husband, wife, parent, child, sibling, or wife of a sibling of the other or the personal representative of any such relative of the other, (d) a member of the household of the other, (e) a business entity, the selection of whose counsel is, as a practical matter and in the given instance, controlled by the other, (f) a person who, as a practical matter and in the given instance, controls the selection of the other's counsel, provided the other is a business entity, or (g) a business entity under direct or indirect common domination with another.

**Part D.** *De Minimus Rule.* If the aggregate of the portions of the originating credits for fees paid by any client that originally were allottable or later become allottable to any individual firm member under the provisions of Parts A, B, and C of these rules is less than one-eighth of the total of such originating credits, such portion shall not be allotted to such individual firm member, but, instead, shall be allotted to the partners.

**Part E.** *Large Client.* Twenty-five percent (25%) of the originating credits attributable to aggregate fees collected from each client (or group of related clients) in excess of $50,000, and an additional 25 percent of the originating credits attributable to aggregate fees collected from each client (or group of related clients) in excess of $100,000, shall be allocated to the partners' fund, and the origination credits of the initial originator or originators reduced proportionately.

**Part F.** *Criminal Case Assignments.* A client whose representation by the firm or a firm member in a criminal matter arose by reason of assignment by a judge or other public official having such authority shall be deemed to have been originated by the firm.

**Part G.** *Law Directory Referrals.* If the event of representation of a client by the firm or a firm member was by reason of the referral from a law list or directory (such as *Martindale-Hubbell*), the client shall be deemed to have been originated by the firm.

# Capitalization, Debt, and Taxes

### by James D. Cotterman

*A*dditional information on this topic is available from the author.

## Capitalization

The modern law firm needs significant amounts of capital. Make that statement and many a lawyer will ask, "Why? We service clients, bill for our services, get paid, and in turn pay our bills. What is the issue?" Not an unreasonable question. Law firms need capital to cover the cash gap that nearly all businesses have. They need capital for growth. Capital is also needed for the technology-driven infrastructure of a modern law firm.

The cash gap in a law firm is the difference between when you pay your expenses and when clients pay you. For law firms, this number is about 105 days. Unbilled time turns over in sixty to seventy days. Accounts receivable turn over in sixty to eighty days. Accounts payable are generally around thirty days. With labor costs—the single largest overhead item (usually paid bi-weekly or semimonthly)—the burden is aggravated because labor's cash gap is closer to 120 days. The recent resurgence of rampant associate wage increases has further compounded the situation.

What this means is that as you operate your business, you are likely to have paid for the services rendered before you have even invoiced the client—hence the need for capital. If you are growing your business, the cash gap is a critical issue to understand. It is possible to grow a business so rapidly that you literally grow it into bankruptcy. Why? Because the growth requires ever-increasing outlays of cash. Meanwhile, the growth in cash receipts lags. If your capital is inadequate, you consume all your cash and you are in trouble.

Think about what happens as you add an associate. On the first day, the associate begins work. Yours is an efficient law firm—the associate is put on billable work fairly quickly. So, by the end of the second week, when the individual receives the first paycheck, he or she is busy on client work. At the end of the month, the second paycheck comes; the associate is still busy. On the first of the second month, benefits begin. In the middle of the second month, the partner returns the prebills to accounting and the third paycheck is issued to the new associate. At the end of the second month, the bill is mailed to the client and the fourth paycheck is issued. By now you can see where this is heading. We are up to four paychecks by the time a bill has gone out (if you are lucky). And we have not even mentioned paying for the laptop computer or other direct marginal costs of the individual, let alone any incremental general overhead. And, of course, you must wait sixty days or so until the client pays. Multiply that cost by inefficiencies along the way, and then again by the number of associates you hire each year.

Now let's talk about technology. Computers that are obsolete after two to four years have replaced the typewriters that used to last twenty years. Worse yet, the typewriters were purchased for only the secretaries and today everyone has a computer (and many have laptops as well). Phone systems are more complex (and expensive). In fact, the entire communication infrastructure of a law firm has changed—phone, fax, voice mail, e-mail, videoconference, the Internet, and integration of voice, data, and video. All these marvels require technology infrastructure and highly skilled (read expensive) people to deploy and manage them. Add in copiers, printers, fax machines, scanners, cell phones, pagers, video projectors, and interoffice communication. And all that requires capital.

Clearly, whether it's business growth, inflation of wages and overhead, technology advances, or credit terms with suppliers and clients, there is a heightened need for capital. The primary sources for capital remain with the owners and their bankers. Landlords help, particularly when they absorb the build-out. The leasing of technology equipment has burgeoned as a means of creating off-balance-sheet financing. But still it comes down to owner investment and banker largesse.

What are the benchmarks used to determine the capital health of a law firm? There are many; some come from the bankers or financial advisors, and some are internally driven by the comfort the owners have with financial leverage. The most common metrics follow:

- Revenues per lawyer
- Revenues per equity partner
- Overhead per lawyer
- Occupancy costs/revenues
- Income per lawyer/revenue per lawyer
- Gross profit margin
- Average equity partner income
- Income per equity partner/revenue per lawyer
- Distributions per equity partner/income per equity partner
- Net cash available for working capital
- Work-In-Progress (WIP) over 180 days/total WIP
- Investment in WIP (# months at year-end)
- Accounts Receivable (AR) over 180 days/total AR
- Invest in AR (# of months at year-end)
- WIP + AR: debt
- Debt per equity partner
- Debt/net fixed assets
- Debt/equity partner compensation
- Total liabilities per equity partner
- Total liabilities/WIP + AR
- Total liabilities/equity partner compensation
- Permanent capital per lawyer
- Permanent capital per equity partner
- Permanent capital/WIP + AR
- Permanent capital/revenues
- Permanent capital/equity partner compensation
- Realization from standard rates
- Leverage (all nonequity partner lawyers: equity partners)
- Billable hours per partner
- Billable hours per associate
- Billable hours per paralegal

In addition, bankers have become more astute at looking more at the business. Questions regarding the nature and stability of partnership structure, governance, management, and client base are common. It is typical for a new relationship to require a five-year history of partners. How many resulted from promotions from the associate ranks, lateral insertions, retirements, competitive withdrawals, and the like? What do the organizational documents say about governance and management? Who occupies these positions and for how long? What are the protocols for owners to buy-in and contribute equity? For clients, the assessment may likely require listing the top twenty to fifty clients (in declining fee revenue) for each of the past five years and indicating the client industry, nature of work, special fee arrangements, and how they came to the firm (yes, bankers understand rainmaking). The patterns of growth or decline, client concentration, and industry concentration are all part of the analysis.

As advisors to the legal profession, Altman Weil advises against borrowing that extends beyond the acquisition of fixed assets. In effect, you should maintain positive equity (capital) on the cash basis. The first law of management is this: do not borrow money to pay the partners or shareholders. The only exception to this law is to zero out profits at year-end in a professional corporation or association. Even then, the debt should be repaid in full by the end of the first quarter of the following year. Working-capital debt should be zero for at least ninety days during the year and at year-end. The former could be achieved by cleaning up the credit line for one week each month.

Law firms are better served when the owners are invested in the firm. Meaningful investment makes one more mindful of the organization's fiscal affairs and more concerned about its competitive position. Such individuals also tend to be more entrepreneurial—a required ingredient for success in a competitive marketplace.

# Debt and Taxes

The preceding discussion on capitalization and borrowing to pay partner compensation raises financial issues; many law firms face potential tax difficulties in this process as well.

### Partnerships

A partner computes taxable income on his or her share of partnership income and the pass-through items of deduction and credit. The partner receives a K-1 from the law firm summarizing this information. The partner does not receive a W-2, as employees do, because a partner is not an employee, but rather is self-employed. The cash distributions a partner receives from the law firm partnership may or may not correlate with the taxable income he or she must report to the Internal Revenue Service.

For example, if a partnership borrows $500,000 and distributes the funds to the partners, the transaction has no income-tax effect for the partnership or the partners. The partners are jointly and severally liable for repayment of the partnership debt. Interest paid for use of the fund is a partnership expense, and hence deductible.

The good news: the partners receive the money free from income taxes. The bad news: when the partnership repays the bank, it uses fee receipts, which normally are used for current operations and partner draws. This reduces the monies available for partner distributions. The repayment of the loan is not a partnership expense. The partners report taxable income on the funds that were paid to the bank. For some partners, the prior-year windfall has already been spent, and the tax bill represents a financial hardship.

## Corporations

If a professional corporation borrows $500,000 and distributes the funds to the shareholders, the payments to the shareholders normally represent compensation that is deductible by the professional corporation and taxable income to the shareholder-employees. The shareholders pay the appropriate federal, state, and local income taxes on the funds. The professional corporation pays interest on the full amount borrowed. Interest is deductible.

Many professional corporations use this technique to eliminate taxable income at year-end. Such actions are necessary because of differing loan amortization and fixed asset depreciation schedules or miscalculations in planning. When used, the funds should be repaid in the first quarter of the following year to minimize interest costs. Until the depreciation and amortization imbalance or other problems reverse, this use of debt will be necessary.

If, however, the borrowed funds were simply an advance against future income, there will come the day of reckoning when the borrowed funds must be repaid, creating taxable income at the corporate level. The worst possible situation could occur where the professional corporation pays federal, state, and local income taxes. The shareholders would not only have reduced current income from the debt repayment, but also the knowledge that the taxing authorities have a significant portion of the original principal. Such use of debt only results in a shifting of taxable income from one year to another, and increases the tax burden drastically, as the borrowed funds were taxed at individual rates and the repaid amounts may be taxed at personal service corporation rates.

# Retirement
# Planning Primer

by James D. Cotterman

Law firms, like all organizations, must deal with the issue of whether current cash should be set aside to provide for the accumulation of retirement assets for their workers. No matter the size of the organization, the potential dollars are substantial.

For law firm owners, the establishment of funded retirement programs represents a direct reduction to the current compensation of the owners. Only plans that provide for individual employee contributions spread the financial impact beyond the ownership group. Note that some firms say that the pension contribution is part of the compensation package and the firm would pay more cash compensation to a nonowner if there were no plan. Altman Weil's experience indicates that the labor market is so competitive that very little, if any, reduction in nonowner cash compensation occurs because of a retirement program.

The intent of this primer is to provide an overview of retirement, discuss the impact of unfunded plans on the profession, encourage further reading on the topic, and stimulate an educational process for all employees. The material is adapted from articles produced by Altman Weil over the years, as well as from data compiled in its surveys of the profession regarding this topic. The primer should begin the process necessary to bring one's plans into line with expectations and economic reality.

Hopefully the age old questions "can I personally afford to retire?" and "can we afford to pay the retirement of others?" can be answered.

## Formal Retirement Policies

Not every law firm has formal documents (such as a partnership agreement or an operating agreement, or their corporate equivalents—articles, bylaws, buy-sell agreements, and employment agreements). Not every agreement speaks to the issue of retirement. The larger the firm, the more likely it has such documentation. Documenting a retirement policy avoids uncertainty and the uncomfortable situation of last-minute, ad hoc, individual negotiations. It also avoids the unfortunate scenario of individual deals spinning out of control.

## Retirement Age

Since 1981, there have been two significant changes in the laws affecting retirement age. The first was the 1986 amendment to the Age Discrimination in Employment Act of 1967 (ADEA), as amended through 1978, which generally prohibits mandatory retirement provisions being applied to employees over the age of forty. The act applies to employers with twenty or more employees. The second change, the Social Security amendments of 1983, gradually increased the age at which full retirement benefits would be available (from sixty-five to sixty-seven) and reduced early retirement benefits over the period from 1983 to 2027. These and other legislative changes acknowledged the "right" and the government's desire that employment continue beyond traditional notions of retirement.

Retirement for the legal profession is not too different from the rest of the economy. Early retirement generally occurs between ages fifty-five (slightly earlier that the nation as a whole) and sixty-two. Normal retirement remains at sixty-five, the traditional retirement age under Social Security. Mandatory retirement is generally between ages sixty-seven and seventy-five, with seventy as the majority choice. Interestingly, just under 50 percent of law firms deal with this issue of retirement age.

## Benefits to Retired Owners

As the baby boom generation marches towards retirement, the topic of postemployment benefits takes on greater importance. Over half of law firms surveyed provide postretirement health insurance. Over two-thirds provide office and staff support and just over one-quarter provide life insurance. In an era of increasing concern over the exploding cost of operating a law firm, it seems that taking care of retired members of the firm is still regarded as the right thing to do.

## Return of Capital

The return of capital in law firms (repurchase of stock in professional corporations) is, for most firms, a minor amount. Less than 10 percent of the firms surveyed indicated that they use the accrual method of valuing capital. Accordingly, the return of capital ranges from a few thousand to a few hundred thousand dollars spread over six to sixty months. This represents two surprising changes from earlier studies. First, that the lower-quartile value for return of capital went from one year to six months; and second, that the upper-quartile value went from three years to five years. The latter probably reflects the increasing number of retirees and the increasing level of capital in many law firms. Unbilled time and accounts receivable generally remain with the law firm. Goodwill is generally not valued. (Given that clients typically hire lawyers and not law firms, that is appropriate.)

## Qualified Retirement Plans

Retirement plans qualified by the Internal Revenue Service (IRS-qualified plans) are practically universal among law firms. Based on earlier studies, smaller law firms have moved in recent years to take greater advantage of these programs.

Professional corporations are created primarily for the tax advantages that come with the corporate form of organization. Central among them are qualified retirement plans. Until 1982, qualified retirement planning for corporations and partnerships had substantial differences. Then, in 1982, the Tax Equity and Fiscal Responsibility Act (TEFRA) eliminated those differences. This allowed significant increases in benefits for proprietorships, partnerships, and S corporations.

Such funded retirement programs—where the availability of retirement assets is assured by setting aside current income as it is earned and before the payment of personal income taxes—had been an absolute winner for many law firms through the mid-1980s. High tax rates and more liberal deferral and exclusion rules made it possible for law firm owners to save more in taxes than contributions for nonowners cost.

The 1986 tax act made the decision more difficult, as the changes in tax and pension laws made it more expensive to maintain such plans. However, the underlying benefit of tax deferral and forced savings in a protected trust continued. Those attributes still represent the single best means to provide for an accumulation of capital for one's later years of life.

Qualified plans are highly regulated under IRS and U.S. Labor Department rules. These plans provide for preferential tax treatment of contributions (immediate deduction) and benefits (tax deferral and special treatment at distribution) in exchange for broad coverage and nondiscrimination provisions. Plan earnings accumulate tax free, and plan assets must be secured (placed outside the reach of the employer and creditors) in a trust for such purpose.

The drawbacks of qualified plans are reporting, disclosure, and other regulatory considerations. Unfortunately, the plans also have severe restrictions on annual contributions and benefits. They are typically expensive to administer, particularly defined-benefit plans, which require the services of actuaries and payment of pension benefit insurance premiums. Also to be considered is the cost of covering nonlawyer employees of the firm. The current coverage and nondiscrimination rules protect employees who are not highly compensated, and prohibit the one-employee professional corporation plans formerly available.

### Qualified Plan Options

What may be confusing is the maze of names: defined benefit, defined contribution, profit sharing, target benefit, 401(k), money purchase, Keogh, and pension plan. A short review of the terms should allow for intelligent review of the options.

There are essentially two forms of organization that law firms utilize: incorporated (professional corporation or association) and unincorporated (sole proprietorship, partnership, and limited liability company). Qualified plans available to corporate forms of organization are corporate plans. Qualified plans for unincorporated businesses are Keogh plans. All plans offer nearly the same features. Keogh plans are based on self-employed earnings, while corporate plans are based on compensation.

There are two main classifications of plans—defined benefit and defined contribution. The names help describe the basic characteristics of each plan.

### Defined-Benefit Plans

Defined-benefit plans specify the benefit that the retiree will receive based on age, years of service, and past earnings. The Pension Benefit Guaranty Corporation (PBGC), a federal agency under the Employee Retirement Income Security Act of 1974 (ERISA), insures the plan assets.[1] Assets of the trust are lumped together, with no individual accounting. Forfeitures remain in the trust to reduce future costs. The benefit can be calculated under several different formulae; unit benefit and flat percentage of earnings (often an average of final earnings) are two common formulae. These plans benefit older individuals, in that they recognize past service and fund for a determined benefit. Such plans are not recommended when the firm does not have a history of—and reasonable prospects for—stable profitability.

Actuaries are needed to establish the funding required to provide adequate reserves from which to pay the retirees. Currently, the maximum benefit for a retiree is the lesser of (1) $160,000 per year (for 2002, indexed to inflation in $5,000 increments), and (2) 100 percent of the average compensation for the three highest consecutive years. The risks of investment performance and inflation lie with the employer (law firm). Accordingly, the cost of funding a plan is not readily determinable without the help of an actuary. You can ensure a significant benefit quickly for older individuals, but often at a high cost. Contributions to the plan are skewed disproportionately toward older individuals with longer service histories. Such a plan can be used effectively to replace unfunded obligations, if its cost is counted as general overhead rather than attributed to the participants.

### Defined-Contribution Plans

Defined-contribution plans focus on individual accounting for contributions. The annual contribution—as opposed to the ultimate benefit—is defined. Accordingly, benefit amounts are neither guaranteed nor insured. The risks of investment performance and inflation lie with the individual. The maximum annual addition to each participant's account is the lesser of 100 percent of compensation or $40,000 (2002, indexed to inflation in $1,000 increments). Because contributions are based on compensation, potential benefits are based on career average earnings. Costs are predictable. These plans work well for younger individuals, who have a lot of time to accumulate retirement funds.

Four types of defined-contribution plans warrant special discussion: money-purchase pension plans, target-benefit plans, profit-sharing plans, and 401(k) plans.

A money-purchase plan has a feature in common with a defined-benefit plan—the annual contribution to the plan is a fixed obligation. Although the obligation is fixed, the calculation of the contribution can be either a fixed percentage of compensation or a fixed dollar amount. These plans are different from defined-benefit plans because the benefit is whatever the *money* will *purchase*.

A target-benefit plan is a hybrid of a defined-benefit plan and a defined-contribution plan, and an extension of a money-purchase plan. The plan is a defined-contribution plan where the contributions are actuarially determined to provide a target benefit. The benefit is not guaranteed; exposure for investment performance and inflation rests with the employee. Essentially, the plan allows for greater funding of benefits for older employees and longer-service employees (owners), while costing less than a true defined-benefit plan or money-purchase plan. This is a great plan to consider for a smaller law firm with senior owners.

A profit-sharing plan is flexible, in that annual contributions by the employer may not be required and amounts can vary. Despite the name, profitability is not required if the profit-sharing plan so states. The law limits total contributions to 25 percent of aggregate employees' compensation (2002 change). A formula determining the allocation of funds to participants must be set forth. Allocations may be integrated with Social Security ("permitted disparity"). Age-weighted profit-sharing plans provide for greater flexibility so that contributions can be based on age in addition to compensation. A further enhancement of age-weighted profit-sharing plans is found with a new breed of plans covered by the following monikers—superintegration, new comparability, or maximum allowable discrimination. Such plans provide for even greater allocation of contributions toward the highly compensated employees. There are some distinct advantages to these plans if you want to take the maximum allocation at the minimum cost.

401(k) plans are very popular. The plan allows a participant to defer current taxation on a portion of his or her annual compensation by making an elective contribution to the plan. The maximum employee contribution is $11,000 for 2002, increasing $1,000 per year until 2006, then indexed in $500 increments. Beginning in 2002, employees who were age fifty or older were allowed to make an additional annual contribution to the plan equal to $1,000 (increased $1,000 each year until 2006, then indexed in $500 increments). These catch-up contributions do not count against section 415(c) limits. Special nondiscrimination rules apply to 401(k) to prevent abuse by highly compensated individuals. Simple 401(k) plans offer the employees of smaller employers (fewer than 100 employees) the ability to contribute up to $7,000 annually (for 2002, increased $1,000 each year to 2005, then indexed in $500 increments). Beginning in 2002, employees who were age fifty or older were allowed to make an additional annual contribution to the plan equal to $500 (increased $500 each year until 2006, then indexed in $250 increments). These catch-up contributions do not count against section 415(c) limits. Top-heavy rules and special nondiscrimination testing for traditional 401(k) plans are avoided.

Simplified employee pension (SEP) plans are not qualified plans; however, they function in many similar ways. Contributions are made to an individual retirement account (IRA) for each employee. The maximum annual contribution is the lesser of 25 percent of compensation and $40,000. There are no catch-up provisions for SEPs. SEPs are administratively simple, and they cost little to maintain. They are designed for this purpose, thus the name—

simplified employee pension. Because contributions go to IRAs, the law firm avoids investment and distribution control and liability. No paperwork is required for termination, and no annual reports are needed. Although contributions are discretionary, participation and vesting requirements are strict.

Many of the titles in qualified retirement plans are used indiscriminately. The following list illustrates the proper family groupings of the various qualified plans available to law firms. Remember that qualified plans for corporations have the same names as Keogh plans (the plans established for unincorporated businesses). Therefore, if someone refers to a Keogh plan, you must ask which one.

1. DEFINED BENEFIT
   - Defined benefit
2. DEFINED CONTRIBUTION
   - Target benefit
   - Money purchase
   - Profit sharing
   - 401(k)
   - SEP
3. PENSION
   - Defined benefit
   - Target benefit
   - Money purchase
4. PROFIT SHARING
   - Profit sharing
   - Age-weighted profit sharing
   - 401(k)

## Nonqualified Retirement Plans

As their name implies, these plans do not qualify for preferential tax treatment under the tax laws (no immediate deduction or tax deferral). Earnings can accumulate tax-free only if a life-insurance product is used. On the other hand, the plans are unhindered by the coverage and nondiscrimination regulations that affect qualified plans. A firm may discriminate, deciding the amount of benefits it is willing to accrue, and for whom. However, these plans must be limited to highly compensated and key management employees. Such programs do not carry the reporting and disclosure burdens of qualified plans (a simple one-time disclosure filing with the U.S. Department of Labor is required). Such plans generally lack the asset security that qualified plans may provide.

The lack of preferential tax treatment (deduction for the employer's contribution must be taken in the same year that the employee recognizes the income) means that it is expensive to fund such plans—they are usually unfunded. Two general funding vehicles exist when the tax cost of funding is not an issue and segregation of the assets is. Rabbi trusts secure the assets for deferred compensation for solvent employers, but not from creditors of insolvent employers. Secular trusts are used when the assets are to be secured from employers' creditors as well. Secular trusts require greater funding than rabbi trusts, because employees must pay taxes on contributions to secular trusts (but not on contributions to rabbi trusts). These funding techniques are common in many corporations, but not in law firms.

# Unfunded Obligations

Traditional unfunded obligations represent a fundamental risk to the legal profession in an era of partner mobility, limited ability to maintain or expand leverage, an aging lawyer population, pricing (cost) constraints from clients, and a very competitive labor market. The history of unfunded obligations goes back to an era before professional corporations, before qualified retirement plans, before ERISA, and, in some cases, before Social Security old-age benefits. It was an era of relatively easy profits, and rapid growth in both lawyers and legal business. Ownership structures were stable. The proportion of the profession benefiting from these obligations was small when compared with the proportion providing the profits from which the benefits were paid.

Unfunded entitlements, which rely on the ability and willingness of future owners to pay the benefits set forth in such plans, continue with some surprising popularity. A little more than 25 percent of law firms maintain such plans. However, the prevalence of these plans has been declining since the late 1980s. And many of the remaining plans have been modified with payment caps, reduced benefit formulas, longer vesting requirements, and other strategies to limit or reduce the future economic impact on the firm.

Today, firms are far more interested in sustainability, succession, and their future viability. If future profits are going to be paid to retired partners, the firm sees the *quid pro quo* as securing future revenue sources in clients and referral sources. Recognizing past service of a partner, except for founders, is just not of prime importance in law firms.

## Social Security Analogy

A large-scale analogy of the legal profession's problem with unfunded obligations is seen in the Social Security system. Social Security was established in 1935 on a pay-as-you-go funding program for retirement. Current workers contribute to the funds as they earn. Benefits for retired, deceased, and disabled workers are paid out of those funds. Active workers' contributions are individually low because of the relationship between the large number of contributors and the vastly smaller number of beneficiaries. In 1946, 8 percent of the U.S. population was age sixty-five or older (eleven million people). Today, 13 percent of the population has reached that milestone (thirty-five million people). By 2030, seventy million people will reach that mark, representing 20 percent of the population.

The lengthening life span of Americans will strain the system. Simply put, beneficiaries are living longer. Life expectancy for a sixty-five-year-old male in 1935 was approximately twelve and one-half additional years, or 16 percent of his life. Today it is seventeen and one-half additional years, or 21 percent of his life. This century is likely to advance that percentage to a full one-third of his life (a life span of nearly 100 years). In all cases, females are expected to live longer, and the life span differences are increasing.

In addition, participation in the workforce has been declining for those between the ages of sixty and sixty-four. In the early 1950s, eighty percent of men between the ages of sixty and sixty-four were working. Today the workforce participation for that group has slipped to fifty percent, and it shows continuing signs of decline. More directly, people are retiring earlier. The consequence is lower contributions and benefits being paid earlier and longer (even if actuarially reduced). The events since 2000 that have affected the nation and the world certainly impact the need to work, particularly for the workforce over age fifty. How that will affect longer-term patterns is yet to be seen.

During the 1980s, the federal government realized that workers would probably be unwilling and unable to afford contributions for the projected benefit stream in the twenty-first century. A solution was designed that combined changes in the calculation of benefit increases, changes in the normal retirement age, and changes in the method of funding for benefits. The funding change provided for increased current contributions, to provide partial reserves to pay for benefits in the twenty-first century. Changes to the system continued during the 1990s. And today, the government continues to wrestle with the political implications and economic solvency of its Social Security and Medicare programs.

## The Legal Profession

The legal profession faces the same demographic issues as the nation generally. The profession is aging. More women are rising through the ranks—at 24 percent of the legal profession in 1995, women could represent 38 percent in another twenty years. The change in the gender mix is particularly important given the statistics on life span for women. There are also indications that the traditional "die with your boots on" ethic is waning.

Moreover, law firms are experiencing burgeoning independence in the lawyer ranks. Both associates and partners are "jumping ship" with increasing frequency. The legal market is extremely competitive, and Model Rule 5.6 of the Model Rules of Professional Conduct (formerly DR 2-108) effectively allows partners and shareholders in law firms to change firms and take their clients with them whenever they choose to do so. As a result, partners or shareholders with books of business that would entitle them to greater compensation elsewhere frequently leave their firms. Often the most productive partners or shareholders defect, along with their revenue streams, which places their firms in severe jeopardy. Left behind in many cases are the liabilities for debt and office space that now must be shared by a smaller group. This is not an environment in which one should entrust one's successors with one's financial retirement entitlements.

Indeed, law firms continue to grapple with past promises and their future economic impact. The answers are not easy, emotions are heightened, and the dollars are not insignificant. But perhaps the most critical agent in why law firms force themselves to deal with the issue is that unfunded retirement and buy-out plans represent a clear competitive disadvantage in the marketplace. Firms seeking senior lateral hires or merger partners have a tough time if the fiscal house is not in order. Good mergers have not happened and attractive lateral candidates have gone elsewhere because of unfunded plans. In a market where finding and keeping the right people is fundamental to the competitive position of the organization, having such a disadvantage is unwise.

A retired partner can generate income from four sources: (1) Social Security benefits, (2) employer (law firm) retirement plans, (3) personal savings and investments, and (4) postretirement employment. In all but the megasize law firms, the second and third sources are essentially the same. If employer-mandated plans are established, however, there is a far greater likelihood that a retiring partner will have financial assets for retirement. Lawyers, like most Americans, often find that maintaining substantial personal savings is a very difficult habit to cultivate.

Many law firms found, however, that the 1986 and subsequent changes in income tax rates have changed the economics of qualified plans. A secondary benefit to deferring taxation of compensation and earnings had historically been that the retiree would most likely be in a lower marginal income tax bracket upon retirement than when the income was earned. The current income tax rate structure makes this less likely. The income tax rate structure at the time of income deferral, the length of time income tax is deferred, and the expected income tax rate structure at distribution affect retirement contribution planning. Current low-income tax rate structures have also increased the cost of covering nonowners, relative to the tax benefit received by partners. Still, many plans can be integrated with Social Security, reducing the costs of covering lower-paid employees.

The historical retirement "plan" had been an income stream for life for retired partners. The modern traditional nonqualified plan consisted of a return of capital and an interest in unbilled time and accounts receivable. Today, most firms with unfunded plans have turned to a percentage of past earnings as the primary valuation of entitlement, in addition to a return of capital. Other primary valuation methods include a percentage or point interest in firm income or a flat dollar amount. Regardless of valuation method, when compared with current partner earnings, the value of the benefit is typically a multiple of one to one and one-half times the individual's earnings. Funding of such plans is rare. However, cost containment caps and service requirements are not. The future for such plans is likely a modest look-back benefit limited to founders and a carefully considered look-forward benefit to sustain critical business relationships.

Many law firm plans that provide for cost containment caps look to limit total benefits paid in any one year. Such limits protect the firm from swings in profitability and the burden of expanding numbers of beneficiaries. Rarely do they limit overall costs.

These plans are often represented by unsecured promises. In essence, the retiree relies on the moral commitment, survival, and financial ability of the firm to honor these agreements. The timing could not be worse if the plans are not viable just when the current group of 35 to 50-old lawyers will be ready for retirement.

## *What to Do*

What should law firms do to deal with this whole area? This depends on what future your firm perceives as rational. Let's assume that having senior partners economically capable of retiring with some reasonable level of income is a prime objective.

First, what are the economics of retiring? Statistically, today's adults will live on average until age eighty-two. However, planners routinely urge more conservative (longer life expectation) planning. Some data indicates that the average life span of at least one member of a retired couple is ninety-three. One may consider it prudent to plan for a life span of ninety to ninety-five years. If not for oneself, then for oneself and spouse combined. We are a much healthier nation today than just a short decade ago—at least we are capable of being healthier. Medical advances continue and the prospects of life spans exceeding

100 years are certainly a consideration in this century. So, to be prudent, let's consider living to age ninety-five as an appropriate planning assumption.

How much money will one need during retirement years? The general rules of thumb suggest two-thirds to three-quarters of your preretirement annual income. Research data indicate that outlays (excluding income taxes and savings) are close to three-quarters of preretirement levels. Many categories fall, but health care becomes more expensive. Again let's assume a conservative posture with 75 percent of preretirement outlays as a prudent planning assumption. Note that we are not talking about income at the moment. Lawyers are generally in the top 5 percent of wage earners, and accordingly there should be considerable excess disposable income in the final years before retirement going towards savings and not outlays. Those final years should portray a healthy balance sheet—no debt. Cash flow should be free of education and support outlays for children, and parents are provided for, if they are still living. Clearly personal circumstances and situation will dictate adjustments to our analysis. For our projections we will use $75,000 in annual outlays. That is just below the Social Security wage base for income and nearly 2.5 times above the average level of outlays for a retired husband and wife.

$75,000 in outlays (or after-tax income) is likely to be approximately $100,000 in pretax income (assuming that Social Security income is $1,500 per month; the rest is unearned income; tax-exempt income is not material to the portfolio; current federal tax rates are used; and a combined state and local income tax rate of 6 percent is provided for). The partner is currently thirty-five years old. To provide for that taxable income from age sixty-five to age ninety-five—a full thirty years or just short of one-third of your entire lifetime—the retiree needs an investment portfolio at retirement (excluding personal property and personal realty) of approximately $4,100,000 if having an estate at age ninety-five is not important, or approximately $7,500,000 if preservation of capital is a goal.

Additional assumptions used in this model are an estimate that preretirement and postretirement inflation will average 3.15 percent annually (the average over the past seventy-six years). To maintain the constant buying power of today's dollars, the retirement income required at age sixty-five is adjusted for inflation, and the then annual retirement income is adjusted each year for inflation during the retirement period. The partner expects to earn a real (inflation adjusted) return of 5.05 percent on preretirement assets. A more conservative 2.85 percent real return is expected postretirement.

The savings required for that amount of money at different ages is shown below. Clearly the earlier one starts saving for retirement, the easier it is. The dramatic difference among the examples reflects the power of compounded returns on the principal over the years. For example, if you set aside $250 each month from age twenty-five to age sixty-five, you will contribute $120,000 of your own money and accumulate approximately $840,000 at an average 8 percent annual return. Forego saving $3,000 at age twenty-five and it is not $3,000 that you keep from your retirement, but rather $62,000. You lose the increase in your final year of savings.

Table A3.1 depicts the cost of delay in dealing with retirement planning. A key assumption for this table is that there are no assets being accumulated for retirement—either in qualified retirement plans or in personal savings. The partner described above delays saving for retirement for ten years while he accumulates possessions, raises children and enjoys the higher income. Notice how much the burden has increased in just ten short years. Well, now college is upon this partner's children and unfortunately, the partner earns too much to qualify for financial aid; only loan programs are available. So another ten years goes by while college is funded and loans are repaid. Now at age fifty-five, the potential burden to accumulate retirement assets is so massive as to suggest that this partner may work very many years beyond initial expectations.

**TABLE A3.1**
**Cost of Delayed Retirement Savings**

| Description | Age 35 | Age 45 | Age 55 |
|---|---|---|---|
| Single lump sum today to provide benefits | $383,000 | $841,000 | $1,850,000 |
| Annual level of contributions required | $ 32,000 | $ 80,400 | $ 257,100 |
| Amount of first contribution if graduated with contributions rising 3.15% annually | $ 23,500 | $ 63,800 | $ 227,200 |

How one saves can be just as important as how much. The use of a qualified retirement plan as the foundation of a retirement savings program offers significant benefits. The assets are secured in a separate trust that is protected from creditors. Contributions to the plan and earnings within the plan receive tax advantages that would not occur if you simply were paid additional compensation. The power of compounded earnings matched with a deferral of income taxes creates a very persuasive argument for utilizing this tool.

Table A3.2 examines the result of saving $40,000 per year for ten years under a qualified plan and in personal savings. It is clear that the qualified plan provides for a significantly higher accumulation that, upon distribution, is subject to tax. Favorable income tax rules, however, may lower or defer the effective tax rate that would otherwise be applied.

**TABLE A3.2**
**Qualified versus Nonqualified Plans**

| Savings Description | Qualified Plan | Nonqualified Plan |
|---|---|---|
| Sum available | $ 40,000 | $ 40,000 |
| Income taxes at 41%* | $ 0 | $ 16,400 |
| Net amount invested | $ 40,000 | $ 23,600 |
| Earnings of 8% on investment | $ 3,200 | $ 1,888 |
| Income taxes at 37% on earnings | $ 0 | $ 774 |
| Net accumulated first year | $ 43,200 | $ 24,714 |
| Approximate at end of ten years | $625,800 | $306,800 |

*Federal income tax rate of 35%, plus estimated state and local income taxes of 6%

## Endnote

1. But if the PBGC steps in to take over a failed plan, the benefits they will provide to retirees are likely to be less than the benefits promised by the employer in the plan.

# *Exempt Employees*

## Meaning of Exempt Status

A federal law, the Fair Labor Standards Act (FLSA), governs wages and hours for employees. Generally, the law contains requirements for minimum wage and overtime pay and recordkeeping, as well as certain protections in child labor and equal pay.

The minimum wage, overtime, recordkeeping, and related provisions under FLSA apply to all employees whose jobs have not been determined to be exempt in status. Whether an employee's job is exempt depends primarily on the nature of the job, the types of duties performed, and the percentage of time engaged in such duties. Also, exempt employees are paid a set salary rather than an hourly wage.

In addition to federal regulations associated with FLSA, state wage-and-hour statutes can affect whether an employee's job is classified as exempt. Expert guidance is recommended for establishing exempt positions, and for designing and administering employee work and benefit policies.

## Categories of Exempt Employees Under FLSA

Law firm managers are primarily concerned with the exemptions from FLSA overtime requirements. The Department of Labor issued a proposal on March 25, 2003 to update the fifty-year-old

FLSA regulations covering overtime pay and exempt status. Published in the Federal Resister on March 31, the proposal set forth broad changes and invited written comments until June 30. Final regulations were to be released in the fall of 2003. Included in the expected revisions is the largest increase in the income threshold for exempt status (below which you are automatically nonexempt) and changes in the definitions and tests for exempt status. The Congress has passed separate bills seeking changes to the issuance of the final regulations. As such, the future of this initiative is unclear. Table A4.1 indicates the current regulations and the proposed changes as they exist in mid-September 2003.

**Table A4.1**
**U.S. Department of Labor Proposal to Strengthen Overtime Protection**

**Side-by-Side Comparison**
The following charts compare the current requirements for exemption from the Fair Labor Standards Act as an executive, administrative, professional, computer, or outside sales employee with the regulations proposed by the Department of Labor.

**Executive Employees**

|  | **Current Long Test** | **Current Short Test** | **Proposed Standard Test** |
|---|---|---|---|
| **Salary** | $155 per week | $250 per week | $425 per week |
| **Duties** | Primary duty of the management of the enterprise or a recognized department or subdivision. | Primary duty of the management of the enterprise or a recognized department or subdivision. | Primary duty of the management of the enterprise or a recognized department or subdivision. |
|  | Customarily and regularly directs the work of two or more other employees. | Customarily and regularly directs the work of two or more other employees. | Customarily and regularly directs the work of two or more other employees. |
|  | Has authority to hire or fire other employees (or recommendations as to hiring, firing, promotion or other change of status of other employees are given particular weight). |  | Has authority to hire or fire other employees (or recommendations as to hiring, firing, promotion or other change of status of other employees are given particular weight). |
|  | Customarily and regularly exercises discretionary powers. |  |  |

| | | |
|---|---|---|
| Does not devote more than 20 percent (40 percent in retail or service establishments) of time to activities that are not directly and closely related to exempt work. | | |

## Administrative Employees

| | Current Long Test | Current Short Test | Proposed Standard Test |
|---|---|---|---|
| **Salary** | $155 per week | $250 per week | $425 per week |
| **Duties** | Primary duty of performing office or non-manual work directly related to management policies or general business operations of the employer or the employer's customers.<br><br>Customarily and regularly exercises discretion and independent judgment.<br><br>Regularly and directly assists a proprietor, or exempt executive or administrative employee; or performs specialized or technical work requiring special knowledge under only general supervision; or executes special assignments under only general supervision.<br><br>Does not devote more than 20 percent (40 percent in retail or service establishments) of time to activities that are not directly and closely related to exempt work. | Primary duty of performing office or nonmanual work directly related to management policies or general business operations of the employer or the employer's customers.<br><br>Customarily and regularly exercises discretion and independent judgment. | Primary duty of performing office or non-manual work directly related to the management or general business operations of the employer or the employer's customers.<br><br>Holds a "position of responsibility" with the employer, defined as either (1) performing work of substantial importance or (2) performing work requiring a high level of skill or training. |

## Learned Professional Employees

| | Current Long Test | Current Short Test | Proposed Standard Test |
|---|---|---|---|
| **Salary** | $170 per week | $250 per week | $425 per week |
| **Duties** | Primary duty of performing work requiring knowledge of an advanced type in a field of science or learning customarily acquired by a prolonged course of specialized intellectual instruction and study.<br><br>Consistently exercises discretion and judgment.<br><br>Performs work that is predominantly intellectual and varied in character and is of such character that the output produced or result accomplished cannot be standardized in relation to a given period of time.<br><br>Does not devote more than 20 percent of time to activities that are not an essential part of and necessarily incident to exempt work. | Primary duty of performing work requiring knowledge of an advanced type in a field of science or learning customarily acquired by a prolonged course of specialized intellectual instruction and study.<br><br>Consistently exercises discretion and judgment. | Primary duty of performing office or non-manual work requiring knowledge of an advanced type in a field of science or learning customarily acquired by a prolonged course of specialized intellectual instruction, but which also may be acquired by alternative means such as an equivalent combination of intellectual instruction and work experience. |

## Creative Professional Employees

| | Current Long Test | Current Short Test | Proposed Standard Test |
|---|---|---|---|
| **Salary** | $170 per week | $250 per week | $425 per week |
| **Duties** | Primary duty of performing work that is original and creative in character in a recognized field of artistic endeavor, and the | Performs work requiring invention, imagination, or talent in a recognized field of artistic endeavor. | Primary duty of performing work requiring invention, imagination, originality, or talent in a recognized field of artistic or creative endeavor. |

result of which depends primarily on the invention, imagination, or talent of the employee.

Consistently exercises discretion and judgment.

Performs work that is predominantly intellectual and varied in character and is of such character that the output produced or result accomplished cannot be standardized in relation to a given period of time.

Does not devote more than 20 percent of time to activities that are not directly and closely related to exempt work.

### Computer Employees

| | Current Long Test | Current Short Test | Section 13(a)(17) Test | Proposed Standard Test |
|---|---|---|---|---|
| **Salary** | $170 per week | $250 per week | $27.63 an hour | $425 per week $27.63 an hour |
| **Duties** | Primary duty of performing work requiring theoretical and practical application of highly specialized knowledge in computer systems analysis, programming, and software engineering.<br><br>Employed as a computer sys- | Primary duty of performing work requiring theoretical and practical application of highly specialized knowledge in computer systems analysis, programming, and software engineering.<br><br>Employed as a computer sys- | Primary duty of (A) application of systems analysis techniques and procedures, including consulting with users, to determine hardware, software, or system functional applications; *or* (B) design, development, documentation, | Primary duty of (A) application of systems analysis techniques and procedures, including consulting with users, to determine hardware, software, or system functional applications; *or* (B) design, development, documentation, |

| | | | |
|---|---|---|---|
| tems analyst, computer programmer, software engineer, or other similarly skilled worker in the computer software field.<br><br>Consistently exercises discretion and judgment.<br><br>Performs work that is predominantly intellectual and varied in character and is of such character that the output produced or result accomplished cannot be standardized in relation to a given period of time.<br><br>Does not devote more than 20 percent of time to activities that are not directly and closely related to exempt work. | tems analyst, computer programmer, software engineer, or other similarly skilled worker in the computer software field.<br><br>Consistently exercises discretion and judgment. | analysis, creation, testing, or modification of computer systems or programs, including prototypes, based on and related to user or system design specifications; *or* (C) design, documentation, testing, creation, or modification of computer programs related to machine operating systems; *or* (D) a combination of duties described in (A), (B), and (C), the performance of which requires the same level of skills.<br><br>Employed as a computer systems analyst, computer programmer, software engineer, or other similarly skilled worker in the computer field. | analysis, creation, testing, or modification of computer systems or programs, including prototypes, based on and related to user or system design specifications; *or* (C) design, documentation, testing, creation, or modification of computer programs related to machine operating systems; *or* (D) a combination of duties described in (A), (B), and (C), the performance of which requires the same level of skills.<br><br>Employed as a computer systems analyst, computer programmer, software engineer, or other similarly skilled worker in the computer field. |

## Outside Sales Employees

| | Current Long Test | Current Short Test | Proposed Standard Test |
|---|---|---|---|
| **Salary** | None required. | None required. | None required. |
| **Duties** | Employed for the purpose of and customarily and regularly engaged away from the employer's place of business in making sales; *or* in obtaining orders or contracts for services or for the use of facilities for which a consideration will be paid by the client or customer.<br><br>Does not devote more than 20 percent of the hours worked by nonexempt employees of the employer to activities that are not incidental to and in conjunction with the employee's own outside sales or solicitations. | No separate "short" test. | Primary duty of making sales; *or* of obtaining orders or contracts for services or for the use of facilities for which a consideration will be paid by the client or customer.<br><br>Customarily and regularly engaged away from the employer's place or places of business. |

# *Benefits*

$\mathbf{P}$robably the hottest topic in employee benefits is the spiraling cost of health care (see the health benefits section below for an update). The following guidelines are assembled from various government and legal profession sources (surveys conducted during the years 1996–2002) as well as Altman Weil's experience and privately conducted surveys. The guidelines cover both lawyers and staff employees and, where noted, indicate differences between small and large firms. Generally, lawyers' benefits are near the upper end of the ranges provided and staff employees' benefits are near the lower end. (For example, the norm shown for vacations is two to three weeks after one year; staff personnel would normally have two weeks, and lawyers three weeks, after one year.) These references are recommended:

- ◆ Association of Legal Administrator's Compensation and Benefits Survey (**http://www.alanet.org**—look under Products, then Financial Management, and scroll down to the Survey). Note that local chapters often conduct their own surveys as well.
- ◆ Bureau of Labor Statistics surveys (**http://www.bls.gov**; surveys can be downloaded in PDF format).

## Time Off

### *Vacations*
- ◆ Two to three weeks after one year
- ◆ Add one week every five to ten years

- Maximum of four to five weeks
- "Use it or lose it" is a common attribute

### Holidays

- No differential based on status
- Seven and one-half to nine and one-half days annually
- Six main holidays (nearly universal): New Year's Day, Memorial Day, Fourth of July, Labor Day, Thanksgiving Day, and Christmas Day
- 66 percent of employers make the Friday after Thanksgiving a holiday
- 50 percent of employers make either Christmas Eve or New Year's Eve a holiday (some give a half-day)
- 33 percent of employers make Presidents' Day or Good Friday a holiday
- 25 percent of employers make Martin Luther King's Birthday a holiday
- 17 percent of employers make Columbus Day or Veterans' Day a holiday

### Sick Time

- Five to fifteen days available after one year
- Add one day every one to five years
- Maximum of ten to thirty days after twenty-five years of service
- Carryover, or pay for unused time, is common

### Other Time Off

- 75 percent of small employers and 90 percent of large employers provide leave for jury duty
- Witness leave is uncommon (though it seems more common with law firms than other types of employers)
- 60 percent of small employers and 80 percent of large employers provide funeral leave
- 25 percent of small employers and 60 percent of large employers provide military leave
- Family leave beyond statutory requirements (see federal Family Medical Leave Act) is very rare

## Health Benefits

### Medical

- Fee-for-service plans declined in popularity throughout 1990s (pricing by underwriters encouraged this trend)

- Preferred-provider organizations (PPOs) are the most common type of plan
- Health maintenance organizations (HMOs) and point-of-service (POS) plans remain solid options

The 1990s began with health care premiums rising at three and one-half times the rate of inflation. By the middle of the decade, the inflation rate and health care premiums were both down, at about 3 percent annually. Then an amazing thing happened—consolidation and competition among plan providers. Health care premium increases actually were lower than inflation and at one point even receded. However, premium increases are on the rebound and are now rising faster than inflation. At the start of 2000, premiums were rising in the 8 percent to 12 percent range over the prior year. Rising prescription drug costs are a primary factor in the increase in health care costs.

According to a 2003 Employee Benefit Research Institute (EBRI) study[1]: "Overall, 19 percent of small employers offering health benefits made changes to their health plan between 2001 and 2002. Sixty-five percent increased deductibles and co-pays; 35 percent switched insurers; 30 percent increased the employee share of the premium; and 29 percent cut back on the scope of benefits. Twenty-six percent increased the scope of benefits."

The average annual health insurance premium in 2000 was $2,655 for single coverage and $6,772 for family coverage in private-sector establishments, an increase of 33.3 percent and 36.7 percent respectively since 1996, according to data from the Agency for Healthcare Research and Quality (AHRQ).[2] Actual costs may be more or less, and depend on plan features and underwriting parameters.

Thirty-two percent of employers paid the full premium for single coverage in 2000. For those employees who contributed to the cost of single coverage, the employee's average monthly contribution was $54.40. Only 19 percent of employers paid the entire premium for family coverage in 2000. For those employees who contributed to the cost of family coverage, the employee's average monthly contribution was $179.75.[3]

## *Dental*

- 80 percent of law firms offer this benefit, with the employer paying on average 60 percent of employee coverage and 24 percent of dependent coverage[4]
- Typical premiums (1999) were between $20 and $25 per month for employee coverage and between $60 and $80 per month for family coverage (actual costs depend on plan features and underwriting parameters)

- Dentists are less likely to accept assignment than doctors, which means employee must pay difference between amount dentist charges and amount plan pays toward usual, customary, and reasonable (UCR) charge

## Retirement Benefits

- Most common retirement program is 401(k) and profit-sharing plan combination
- Defined-benefit plans declined in prevalence throughout 1990s
- 71 percent of plans permit loans
- 58 percent of employers pay plan adminsitration expenses outside of the plan
- 50 percent of plans provide for an employer match on 401(k) contributions by employees
- 31 percent of plans have permitted disparity with Social Security wage base

## Other Benefits (Ranked by Frequency)

Provided by more than 50 percent of employers:

- Life insurance (group term: flat amount or multiple of compensation, sometimes capped at $50,000 because of U.S. tax laws, general range of $5,000 to $25,000 if stated and 1.5 times if multiple)
- Long-term disability (generally a 90- to 180-day waiting period; definition and duration of "your occupation" are critical factors)
- Accidental death and dismemberment (equal to life coverage for death and stated percentage for dismemberment)
- FSA or cafeteria (particularly for dependent care, medical expense, and premium conversion)
- Short-term disability (often self-insured)
- Parking and mass-transit subsidies

Provided by less than 50 percent of employers:

- Vision benefits (eye examinations, prescription glasses, and contact lenses) insured, self-insured, or both
- Tuition reimbursement
- Annual physical examinations
- Health clubs

## Endnotes

1. Employee Benefit Research Institute, **http://www.ebri.org/**.

2. Agency for Healthcare Research and Quality, *Health Insurance Premiums Rose More Than 30 Percent Between 1996 and 2000* (Press release, September 12, 2002), **http://www .ahrq.gov/news/press/pr2002/insprepr.htm**.

3. U.S. Department of Labor Bureau of Labor Statistics, *Employee Benefits in Private Industry* (2000).

4. *2002 Compensation and Benefits Survey* (Lincolnshire, IL: Association of Legal Administrators, September 2002).

# *Deciding Who's Right (and Who's Wrong) for Your Law Firm*

by Thomas S. Clay

**W**hen asked about their primary focus, most law firm managing partners would probably say profitability or growth. When queried about the business factor that most concerns them, they might cite increasing competition. But if you probed more deeply to learn what managing partners actually spend the bulk of their time on, the answer you would hear most often is people.

The examples are familiar: the 900-pound-gorilla partner who terrorizes associates; an able and senior lawyer who is a disaster as a practice group leader; the unproductive partner who no one has the stomach to let go; or the clash of cultures in a newly merged firm. These are the issues that law firm leaders struggle with—the issues that ultimately get in the way of building a more competitive law firm.

In our consulting engagements, Altman Weil is called upon to help law firms in many different areas, and yet it is striking how often we find that the root of the problem is the same—people. The right people in the wrong jobs, the wrong people in the partnership, and a lack of awareness or will to solve the problem.

## "First Who . . . Then What"

Our longstanding belief that identifying and solving people issues is a critical foundational step for building successful law firms has been reinforced by a recent study of success in corporate America. In his highly-acclaimed 2001 book, *Good to Great*, author Jim Collins found that companies that want to go from being simply good to being great must decide "first who . . . then what."

Collins states, "First get the right people on the bus (and the wrong people off the bus) before you figure out where to drive it." In other words, before all else, including strategic planning, mission implementation, or organizational strategy, determine *who* should be part of your organization.

> **UNRESOLVED "PEOPLE PROBLEMS" CAUSE REAL DAMAGE**
>
> The managing partner of a multi-office, 150-lawyer firm called us recently to discuss several issues. Finally he said, "We have eight to twelve people that we just can't get rid of and we need help." The problem had festered over many months and enormous management time was being absorbed. Some highly productive partners had already left the firm, despairing that the "bad apples" would never be dealt with.

Additionally, Collins advocates exercising "sheer rigor" in an organization's decision-making and implementation processes where they involve people. Be rigorous, he advises, but not ruthless.

Collins's elegant articulation of these principles should be considered by all good law firms striving to become great.

## Current Market Realities

In 2003, many law firms will attempt to become more competitive through strategic planning, marketing or reorganization, and they will not be wrong to do so. But they will be only half right, unless they also address critical people issues head-on. Having the right people in the firm (and only the right people) is not a luxury. It is a necessity.

Here are some factors to consider:

- ◆ The proliferation of law firm mergers, acquisitions, and lateral recruitment means that firms are constantly adding to and changing their lawyer mix. In the past, law firm cultures were built through slow, steady growth. Associates were evaluated and reviewed for seven years to ensure a fit with the firm. In today's environment, new people are added all the time—people who have an immediate impact on the culture. As firms employ these new methods of growth, they should be increasingly rigorous about identifying problem people and dealing with them expeditiously.

◆ Law firm recruiting and training strategies are more important than ever. With the cost of losing an associate approaching $250,000, firms cannot afford too many mistakes in hiring and retention.

◆ There are certain types of law practices that simply don't fit together well. When the critical success factors for such practices are in conflict, firms must make not only strategic decisions about service mix, but decisions regarding who should stay and who should go.

◆ Many firms have made partners of people who should not be partners. We are seeing a trend toward de-equitizing or installing tiered partnerships and other strategies to deal with this problem. But these strategies are just Band-Aids, often resulting in the wrong people remaining—just in different seats.

◆ The recent economic slump has resulted in layoffs throughout the profession. In some instances the right people were let go and the wrong people retained.

## Why It's Harder for Law Firms

There are unique organizational and structural differences in law firms that make implementation of a rigorous personnel-screening strategy more challenging than in other businesses. That is not to say that firms should shy away from such implementation, only that they should be aware that these differences will shape the way the issues are addressed and recognize that there will be some speed-bumps along the way. Here are some of the salient differences.

◆ Lawyers, unlike executives in industry, have multiple roles in the organization including

### THE 900-POUND GORILLA

A practice group leader, with whom we worked and who was the leader of the firm's largest and most profitable group, literally begged his executive committee to get rid of "my major headache," as he put it. The committee refused because the partner controlled $750,000 of business. As the practice group leader lamented later, "If I didn't have to spend all my time cleaning up all Bob's messes and could focus on opportunities instead, we could be twice as profitable."

salesperson, producer, manager, and owner. This makes development of the correct profile of who should be "on the bus" much more difficult.

◆ Although many firms are organized as business corporations, they still operate like fraternal partnerships. Lawyers like the idea that many, if not all, important decisions are made by the partners. Often responsibility is delegated to management without sufficient concomitant authority.

◆ Autonomy is generally held as a value among lawyers. Lawyers like to be left alone to do as they wish and lawyer leaders often are reluctant to operate differently. Making decisions about people and being rigorous in implementation is extremely difficult when autonomy is valued so highly.

◆ In industry, getting an executive "off the bus" seldom leads to a direct reduction in revenues. In law firms it almost always does. This is a serious dilemma if the person who happens to be a "wrong person" is also a heavy producer of legal work or generator of new business.

◆ Corporations have policies, systems, and procedures as well as human resources departments to assure humane treatment in dealing with people. Law firms are often ill equipped to do so (although they usually want to). This often leads to avoiding problems altogether.

## Laying the Groundwork

Three conditions must be in place for a firm to address people issues successfully.

First, there must be agreement about the firm's operating policy among the partners about recruiting and retaining only those people who meet the definition (profile) of who should be part of the firm. Based on long experience, we recommend a collective decision on this policy, no matter how large the firm. Retreats, focus groups, and informal roundtables are excellent ways to create the agreement.

Second, a profile of characteristics that describe the right people must be developed. There is no universal profile for law firms. Firms must define their own set of values, nonnegotiable behaviors, and contributions required to keep one's seat on the bus. A majority of partners should endorse the profile—but it should not require unanimity.

Finally, a clear, equitable policy must be established to assure that firm leadership can be rigorous in evaluating people against the profile and dealing with these who need to leave or be moved into a new role in the firm.

# Creating the Profile

Altman Weil has organized numerous management retreats around these principles and our experience is that the most challenging part of dealing with the "first who . . . then what" process is defining who fits.

The simple idea of a wrong person is a difficult concept in many firms. Wrong in a law firm usually means incompetent or substandard lawyering skills, ethical behavior, or productivity. While these standards certainly might comprise part of the profile, other characteristics may render a person wrong for the firm. For example, a fundamental disagreement over the firm's mission or vision, a disagreement related to values, a dispute about the need for accountability, or disagreements over how to compensate people might also constitute wrong behavior.

Wrong does not mean bad, but more often represents an irresolvable disagreement over fundamental issues. It relates to a person's willingness to conform to the majority for the good of the firm. This operating concept *does not* mean that legitimate differences cannot exist, or that they should not be brought forward and debated.

Many law firms view creating the profile as an economically oriented exercise calculated to prune dead wood. While personal economic viability is often a part of the profile, firms should not assume that the screening process relies *only* on economic parameters.

In fact, in *Good to Great*, Collins specifically advises against using this process as "an excuse for mindlessly chopping out people to improve performance." We see firms today doing precisely this—often to improve publicly stated net income per partner.

> ## THE UNDERPRODUCTIVE PARTNER
>
> **How about the lawyer who does everything right in terms of team play, following firm policy and procedures, but chooses to work only 1,200 hours per year, when the norm is 1,800? Should this lawyer continue to be a member of the firm?**

Probably the most important lesson for law firms is that although sometimes the wrong people are economically productive, in spite of their productivity they should not be in the firm. This is often the hardest thing to be rigorous about. Alternatively, some under-productive people may be the right people who are simply in the wrong seats and it is up to leadership to figure out where they fit in the firm.

Our work has shown that there is no "right" profile for every firm. A highly entrepreneurial firm may have one set of needs, values, and contribution requirements, whereas an old-line institutional firm will likely have a different set of requirements. The challenge is to figure out what *your* firm needs.

You might begin with these basic standards that we have found most firms agree upon:

- Professional and technical competence
- Accountability for upholding the (particular) firm's values, in all respects
- Contribution in *all* the ways required of the firm's partners

An expanded definition of each of these three *tailored to your firm* could comprise the standards to which everyone in the firm should be held. Once established, management can use this profile to determine whether individuals are right or wrong for your organization.

## Evaluating People

Most firms have some type of performance review program for associate lawyers. Such programs are excellent vehicles for spotting problem people early on and dealing with them. Some firms have annual performance, compensation, or even peer reviews for partners. These are excellent systems for aligning expectations, discussing strengths and weaknesses, and setting professional development goals. However, these processes are probably *not* the best means of dealing with people who are judged wrong for the firm.

In any firm, there are relatively few people who simply do not fit and they are usually easy for management to identify. Practice leaders and senior management know who they are.

### THE MALCONTENT

Associate Sue is technically as good as they come. She is excellent with clients and they like her. But within the firm, she is insatiable and can focus on nothing but her compensation. It is the focus of every conversation with partners, associates, and support staff. Sue likes to measure her compensation against associates from other firms and there is speculation that she is providing firm compensation information to www.GreedyAssociates.com. Should she remain with the firm?

However, firm leaders must challenge themselves not to look the other way or to rationalize negative behavior and allow a wrong person to remain. Jim Collins suggests two simple but useful questions that can initiate the evaluation process:

♦ If you were faced with a hiring decision (rather than a "should this person get off the bus?" decision), would you hire the person again?

♦ If the person came to tell you that he or she was leaving to pursue an exciting new opportunity, would you feel terribly disappointed or secretly relieved?

Senior management should periodically ask practice leaders to identify people they believe do not fit, and then to articulate why, using the agreed-upon profile as a standard. This is a simple but highly effective process that results in a close collaboration among leadership who will make the decision, rigorously but humanely. Once someone has been identified, the process of outplacement should start immediately.

## Right People, Wrong Seats

An important element of the people-evaluation process is determining whether people who clearly should be in the firm are occupying the right positions. This means determining whether each person is employing his or her greatest strengths in the best manner for the firm. This is management at the most basic level–proper allocation of resources.

Broadly defined, the seats for lawyers in a law firm are:

♦ Producers of work
♦ Managers and leaders
♦ Salespeople

Most of the conflicts or right-seat problems in law firms revolve around management and leadership positions. This is because firms often assign or elect people to positions for the wrong reasons. Instead of focusing on a person's demonstrated management or leadership skills, the firm looks at legal skills, rainmaking, or

### THE RIGHT PERSON IN THE WRONG SEAT

Consider the practice leader who is billing in excess of 2,400 hours per year and markets energetically. He's terribly upset that no one else in the group works as hard as he does. When he developed a plan for the group (over an entire weekend) and got lukewarm feedback, he asked us to help "solve the problem." Conversations with group members showed that the group leader was enormously respected as a lawyer and producer of business, but as one member stated, "Jim doesn't have a clue about managing or leading professionals, but his ego probably wouldn't allow anyone else to manage while he did what he does best."

seniority as being the appropriate qualifications. The erroneous assumption that the skills that make an excellent lawyer or rainmaker necessarily equate to being an effective manager leads to having the right people in the wrong seats.

Perhaps the greatest struggle facing law firm leadership currently is having the wrong people in practice group leadership roles. Many managing partners (or executive committees) struggle with what to do with a highly regarded *lawyer* who does not have the skills to be an effective manager or leader.

Moving people to other seats is often more trying than getting someone off the bus altogether. Political realities, a dearth of skilled managers, emotions, and relationships all combine to make the job difficult. Nevertheless, having resources poorly employed can be as debilitating as allowing the wrong people to remain with the firm.

It is important to articulate reasons why a person is ill placed. Why is the person wrong for the seat they occupy?

Is it because:

◆ They don't have the skills to do the job well?
◆ They were placed for political reasons?
◆ They wanted the position for the wrong reasons?
◆ They don't spend the time needed to do the job well?
◆ They do not command the necessary respect from peers?

You can answer these questions through observation, investigation, and testing for personality and skills.

Savvy managing partners know the best way to get people to move seats is to get *them* to recognize that they are not properly placed. A focus on how a person could use his or her skills better (in another position) is the best way to begin such conversations. Beginning with an assessment of weaknesses is likely to evoke denial, defensiveness, and counter attacks. A strategy of multiple progressive meetings has proven best in these circumstances.

## When People Just Don't Fit

Discipline in execution–"rigor" as Collins says–must accompany the decision about people. Unless you translate decisions into concrete actions, no useful change occurs. Speed and process integrity are key. The following has been helpful in those firms that manage the process well:

1. Inform colleagues and others who may be affected by the change, educating them about the "right people" operating philosophy.

2. Inform the person and, at the same time, initiate the humane process, which may include several steps such as severance packages, outplacement assistance, and so on.

3. Communicate quickly and accurately with those who remain and have the closest ties to the individual.

## An Investment Worth Making

Lawyers often use the term collegiality to describe the ideal working environment. More often than not this is code for their strong desire for autonomy combined with an equally strong disinclination for any accountability to the organization. As one lawyer put it recently, "Why should we care about anyone's behavior as long as they produce 2,200 billable hours?" The naiveté of that statement is astounding, but not all that far from the thinking of many lawyers. It brings to mind the image of thoroughbreds racing across the fields in a dozen different directions . . . *power without focus.*

Law firms, like all organizations, can benefit from the enormous power of professionals working in concert. Individuals who choose not to use their skills and strength to further the goals of the organization eventually will become an obstacle or a detriment to it. Only when your firm has made and implemented the tough decisions to get rid of the wrong people and realign the right ones in the most appropriate roles will you be able to harness the full energies of the firm for meaningful change. Then you can, as Collins suggests, "put your best people on your biggest opportunities, not your biggest problems."

The benefits will be enormous.

# Index

# Selected Finance Books from . . .
# THE ABA LAW PRACTICE MANAGEMENT SECTION

## How to Draft Bills Clients Rush to Pay, Second Edition

By J. Harris Morgan and Jay G Foonberg

Spend an hour or two with noted law practice management authorities Morgan and Foonberg as they take you step by step through the process of building the client relationship, setting the appropriate fee agreement, and drafting the bill that will get you paid. You'll find, in plain language, a rational and workable approach to creating fee agreements and bills that satisfy your clients, build their trust, and motivate them to pay. Comparisons and samples of fee agreements and invoices are integrated throughout the text, along with a clear explanation of which methods work best—and why.

## How to Start and Build a Law Practice, Platinum Fifth Edition

By Jay G Foonberg

This classic ABA Bestseller—no completely updated—is the primary resource for starting your own firm. This acclaimed book covers all aspects of getting started, including finding clients, determining the right location, setting fees, buying office equipment, maintaining an ethical and responsible practice, maximizing available resources, upholding your standards, and marketing your practice, just to name a few. In addition, you'll find a business plan template, forms, checklists, sample letters, and much more. A must for any lawyer just starting out—or growing a solo practice.

## Results-Oriented Financial Management: A Step-By-Step Guide to Law Firm Profitability, Second Edition

By John G. Iezzi, CPA

This hands-on, how-to book will assist managing partners, law firm managers, and law firm accountants by providing them with the budgeting and financial knowledge they need to need to make the critical decisions. Whether you're a financial novice or veteran manager, this book will help you examine every facet of your financial affairs from cash flow and budget creation to billing and compensation. Also included with the book are valuable financial models on CD-ROM allowing you to compute profitability and determine budgets by inputting your own data. The appendix contains useful forms and examples from lawyers who have actually implemented alternative billing methods at their firms.

## Collecting Your Fee: Getting Paid From Intake to Invoice.

By Edward Poll

This practical and user-friendly guide provides you with proven strategies and sound advice that will make the process of collecting your fees simpler, easier, and more effective! This handy resource provides you with the framework around which to structure your collection efforts. You'll learn how you can streamline your billing and collection process by hiring the appropriate staff, establishing strong client relationships from the start, and issuing client-friendly invoices. In addition, you'll benefit from the strategies to use when the client fails to pay the bill on time and what you need to do to get paid when all else fails. Also included is a CD-ROM with sample forms, letters, agreements, and more for you to customize to your own practice needs.

## Winning Alternatives to the Billable Hour: Strategies That Work, Second Edition

Edited by James A. Calloway and Mark A. Robertson

In this new and updated Second Edition, you'll find out how to initiate and implement different billing methods that make sense for you and your client. You'll learn how to explain—clearly and persuasively—the economic and client service advantages in changing billing methods. You'll discover how to establish a win-win billing situation with your clients no matter which method you choose. Written for lawyers in firms of all sizes, this book provides valuable examples, practical tools, and tips throughout. The appendix contains numerous useful fee letters, agreements, and other resources—many of which are also provided on the accompanying diskette.

## Billing Innovations: New Win-Win Ways to End Hourly Billing

By Richard C. Reed

If you are trying to decide how to implement a changed approach to billing and pricing, this book will guide you through some of the most important concepts and techniques that cutting-edge law firms are using successfully. You'll learn how billing and pricing are intertwined with other functions of an efficient law practice. Chapters are supported with helpful checklists, self-assessment questionnaires, sample attorney-client and legal services agreements, and guidelines for selecting a billing method.

## Anatomy of a Law Firm Merger:
## How to Make or Break the Deal, Third Edition
By Hildebrandt International
How can you effectively navigate the merger process? This updated Third Edition can help you decide when to consider a merger and how to make the many other decisions involved in completing the merger and ultimately integrating the merged firm. This resource will help you to consider the right and wrong reasons to merge, analyze strengths and weaknesses, and formulate specific goals for the merger. The book also contains valuable exhibits, questionnaires, and checklists—furnished in text and CD-ROM formats.

## Unbundling Legal Services:
## A Guide to Delivering Legal Services a la Carte
By Forrest S. Mosten
Unbundling, the practice of supplying the client discrete lawyering tasks according to the client's direction, is changing the face of the legal profession today. Given minor modifications, any firm can start unbundling their law practice and offer this new consumer-oriented approach to legal service delivery to their clients. Learn how to set up and manage an unbundling law practice, get new clients, and market this new area of your practice. Offered as a supplement to a traditional full-service practice, you will recapture market share and gain professional satisfaction by offering this innovative service.

## The Essential Formbook:
## Comprehensive Management Tools for Lawyers
## Volume I: Partnership and Organizational Agreements/Client Intake and Fee Agreements
## Volume II: Human Resources/Fees, Billing, and Collection
## Volume III: Calendar and File Management/ Law Firm Financial Analysis
By Gary A. Munneke and Anthony E. Davis
Useful to legal practitioners of all specialties and sizes, these volumes will help you establish profitable, affirmative client relationships so you can avoid unnecessary risks associated with malpractice and disciplinary complaints. And, with all the forms available on CD-ROM, it's easy to modify them to match your specific needs. Visit our Web site at www.lawpractice.org/catalog/511-0424 for more information about this invaluable resource.

## The ABA Guide to Lawyer Trust Accounts
By Jay G Foonberg
Avoid the pitfalls of trust account rules violations! Designed as a self-study course or as seminar materials, with short, stand-alone chapters that walk you through the procedures of client trust accounting, this indispensable reference outlines the history of applicable ethics rules; how you could inadvertently be violating those rules and exposing yourself to discipline even where no one is harmed; ways to work with your banker and accountant to set up the office systems you need to avoid trust account problems; numerous forms that you can adapt for your office (including self-tests for seminars and CLE credits); plus Foonberg's "10 rules of good trust account procedures" and "10 steps to good trust account records"—intended to work with whatever local rules your state mandates.

## Flying Solo: A Survival Guide for the Solo Lawyer, Third Edition
Edited by Jeffrey R. Simmons
More and more lawyers, both new and seasoned, are opting to start their own practice. This book will give solos—as well as small firms—all the information needed to build a successful practice. Significantly expanded and completely updated from the previous edition, this book contains 55 chapters written by authorities nationwide on topics such as how to make the decision to go solo, determine the best kind of practice, handle money issues, choose a location for your office, work with other professionals, organize and run your business, manage billing and cash flow, choose computers and equipment, and much more. Cutting-edge issues including Web ethics, telecommuting, and the best technology for a solo or small office success of the firm are also covered.

LawPracticeManagementSection
MARKETING • MANAGEMENT • TECHNOLOGY • FINANCE

## TO ORDER CALL TOLL-FREE:
## 1-800-285-2221

## VISIT OUR WEB SITE:
## www.lawpractice.org/catalog

# 30-Day Risk-Free Order Form
## Call Today! 1-800-285-2221
### Monday–Friday, 7:30 AM – 5:30 PM, Central Time

| Qty | Title | LPM Price | Regular Price | Total |
|---|---|---|---|---|
| _____ | How to Draft Bills Clients Rush to Pay, Second Edition (5110495) | $ 57.95 | $ 67.95 | $_____ |
| _____ | How to Start and Build a Law Practice, Platinum Fifth Edition (5110508) | 57.95 | 69.95 | $_____ |
| _____ | Results-Oriented Financial Management, Second Edition (5110493) | 89.95 | 99.95 | $_____ |
| _____ | Collecting Your Fee: Getting Paid From Intake to Invoice  (5110490) | 69.95 | 79.95 | $_____ |
| _____ | Winning Alternatives to the Billable Hour, Second Edition (5110483) | 129.95 | 149.95 | $_____ |
| _____ | Billing Innovations: New Win-Win Ways to End Hourly Billing (5110366) | 124.95 | 144.95 | $_____ |
| _____ | Anatomy of a Law Firm Merger, Third Edition (5110506) | 79.95 | 94.95 | $_____ |
| _____ | Unbundling Legal Services (5110448) | 54.95 | 64.95 | $_____ |
| _____ | The Essential Formbook: Volume I (5110424V1) | 169.95 | 199.95 | $_____ |
| _____ | The Essential Formbook: Volume II (5110424V2) | 169.95 | 199.95 | $_____ |
| _____ | The Essential Formbook: Volume III (5110424V3) | 169.95 | 199.95 | $_____ |
| _____ | The ABA Guide to Lawyer Trust Accounts (5110374) | 69.95 | 79.95 | $_____ |
| _____ | Flying Solo, Third Edition (5110463) | 79.95 | 89.95 | $_____ |

**\*Postage and Handling**

| | |
|---|---|
| $10.00 to $24.99 | $5.95 |
| $25.00 to $49.99 | $9.95 |
| $50.00 to $99.99 | $12.95 |
| $100.00 to $349.99 | $17.95 |
| $350 to $499.99 | $24.95 |

**\*\*Tax**
DC residents add 5.75%
IL residents add 8.75%
MD residents add 5%

| | |
|---|---|
| Subtotal | $_____ |
| *Postage and Handling | $_____ |
| **Tax | $_____ |
| TOTAL | $_____ |

## PAYMENT

❑ Check enclosed (to the ABA)

❑ Visa     ❑ MasterCard     ❑ American Express

_____
Account Number     Exp. Date     Signature

Name _____  Firm _____
Address _____
City _____  State _____  Zip _____
Phone Number _____  E-Mail Address _____

## Guarantee
If—for any reason—you are not satisfied with your purchase, you may return it within 30 days of receipt for a complete refund of the price of the book(s). No questions asked!

**Mail: ABA Publication Orders, P.O. Box 10892, Chicago, Illinois 60610-0892**
**♦ Phone: 1-800-285-2221 ♦ FAX: 312-988-5568**

**E-Mail: abasvcctr@abanet.org ® Internet: http://www.lawpractice.org/catalog**

# CUSTOMER COMMENT FORM

Title of Book: _____

We've tried to make this publication as useful, accurate, and readable as possible. Please take 5 minutes to tell us if we succeeded. Your comments and suggestions will help us improve our publications. Thank you!

1. How did you acquire this publication:

☐ by mail order          ☐ at a meeting/convention          ☐ as a gift

☐ by phone order        ☐ at a bookstore                         ☐ don't know

☐ other: (describe) _____
_____

Please rate this publication as follows:

|  | Excellent | Good | Fair | Poor | Not Applicable |
|---|---|---|---|---|---|
| **Readability**: Was the book easy to read and understand? | ☐ | ☐ | ☐ | ☐ | ☐ |
| **Examples/Cases**: Were they helpful, practical? Were there enough? | ☐ | ☐ | ☐ | ☐ | ☐ |
| **Content**: Did the book meet your expectations? Did it cover the subject adequately? | ☐ | ☐ | ☐ | ☐ | ☐ |
| **Organization and clarity**: Was the sequence of text logical? Was it easy to find what you wanted to know? | ☐ | ☐ | ☐ | ☐ | ☐ |
| **Illustrations/forms/checklists**: Were they clear and useful? Were there enough? | ☐ | ☐ | ☐ | ☐ | ☐ |
| **Physical attractiveness**: What did you think of the appearance of the publication (typesetting, printing, etc.)? | ☐ | ☐ | ☐ | ☐ | ☐ |

Would you recommend this book to another attorney/administrator? ☐ Yes ☐ No

How could this publication be improved? What else would you like to see in it?
_____
_____
_____

Do you have other comments or suggestions? _____
_____
_____

Name _____
Firm/Company _____
Address _____
City/State/Zip _____
Phone _____
Firm Size: _____ Area of specialization: _____

**We appreciate your time and help.**

Fold

## BUSINESS REPLY MAIL

FIRST CLASS     PERMIT NO. 16471     CHICAGO, ILLINOIS

*. POSTAGE WILL BE PAID BY ADDRESSEE*

AMERICAN BAR ASSOCIATION
PPM, 8th FLOOR
750 N. LAKE SHORE DRIVE
CHICAGO, ILLINOIS 60611–9851

Fold

**JOIN the ABA Law Practice Management Section (LPM) and receive significant discounts on future LPM book purchases! You'll also get direct access to marketing, management, technology, and finance tools that help lawyers and other professionals meet the demands of today's challenging legal environment.**

## Exclusive Membership Benefits Include:

- **Law Practice Magazine**
  Eight annual issues of our award-winning *Law Practice* magazine, full of insightful articles and practical tips on Marketing/Client Development, Practice Management, Legal Technology, and Finance.
- **ABA TECHSHOW®**
  Receive a $100 discount on ABA TECHSHOW, the world's largest legal technology conference!
- **LPM Book Discount**
  LPM has over eighty titles in print! Books topics cover the four core areas of law practice management – marketing, management, technology, and finance – as well as legal career issues.
- **Law Practice Today**
  LPM's unique web-based magazine in which the features change weekly! Law Practice Today covers all the hot topics in law practice management *today* – current issues, current challenges, current solutions.
- **Discounted CLE & Other Educational Opportunities**
  The Law Practice Management Section sponsors more than 100 educational sessions annually. LPM also offers other live programs, teleconferences and web cast seminars.
- **LawPractice.news**
  This monthly eUpdate brings information on Section news and activities, educational opportunities, and details on book releases and special offers.

## *Complete the membership application below.*

### Applicable Dues:
o$40 for ABA members          o$5 for ABA Law Student Division members

**(ABA Membership is a prerequisite to membership in the Section.  To join the ABA, call the Service Center at 1-800-285-2221.)**

### Method of Payment:
oBill me          Charge to my:          oVisa          oMasterCard          oAmerican Express

Card number _____ Exp. Date _____

Signature _____ Date _____

### Applicant's Information (please print):
Name _____ ABA I.D. number _____

Firm/Organization _____

Address _____ City/State/Zip _____

Telephone _____ FAX_____ Email _____

**Fax your application to 312-988-5528 or join by phone: 1-800-285-2221, TDD 312-988-5168**
**Join online at www.lawpractice.org.**

I understand that my membership dues include $16 for a basic subscription to *Law Practice Management* magazine. This subscription charge is not deductible from the dues and additional subscriptions are not available at this rate. Membership dues in the American Bar Association and its Sections are not deductible as charitable contributions for income tax purposes but may be deductible as a business expense.